Building Better Citizens

Building Better Citizens

A New Civics Education for All

Holly Korbey

ROWMAN & LITTLEFIELD
Lanham • Boulder • New York • London

Published by Rowman & Littlefield
An imprint of The Rowman & Littlefield Publishing Group, Inc.
4501 Forbes Boulevard, Suite 200, Lanham, Maryland 20706
www.rowman.com

6 Tinworth Street, London SE11 5AL

British Library Cataloguing in Publication Information Available

Library of Congress Control Number: 2019949767

∞ ™ The paper used in this publication meets the minimum requirements of American
National Standard for Information Sciences Permanence of Paper for Printed Library
Materials, ANSI/NISO Z39.48-1992.

O, let America be America again—
The land that never has been yet—
And yet must be—the land where every man is free.
—Langston Hughes, "Let America Be America Again"

I want a democracy so compelling even the children will want to try it.
—John Harris Loflin

Contents

Acknowledgments

Though my name appears on this book's cover, it would not exist without the help and contributions of so many people, and I'm overflowing with gratitude to all of them. First and foremost, thank you to my husband Chris and my three sons Holden, Zane, and Adrian, who ran our household while I spent my evenings revising chapters at Starbucks. I owe endless thanks to my mom, my dad, and my sister Annie for sitting through violin lessons and Little League practices with my kids so I could write. The same goes for my parenting tribe, especially Erin and Dave Merryman, Will and Abby Humphrey, and Lissa Smith, who helped me on an unbelievable number of occasions. These people have cooked dinners and played board games, sat in carpool lines and aided with homework, all to make this book happen.

I'm so lucky to have worked with wonderful people on the book, especially the amazing Sarah Jubar at Rowman & Littlefield, the editor who first saw the potential in a book about a civics education revival and then took me from first ideas to the finish line, and editor Catherine Herman's eye for detail. I also owe so much gratitude to my editor and friend Nora Fleming, who read early drafts and gifted me with her supreme organizational insight, and editor and friend Ki Sung, who really knows how to talk a writer off the ledge, even from the other side of the country.

This book also benefited greatly from many experts with inside knowledge of different aspects of civics education, and for that I thank Peter Levine, Robert Pondiscio, Kei Kawashima-Ginsberg, Ted McConnell, Tony Wagner, and Mike Caulfield for their expert advice and guidance, and for patiently addressing too many emails, explaining a data point to me for the tenth (or the hundredth) time. The Education Writers Association's conference on civics and citizenship, which I attended through their generous financial support, provided me with knowledgeable sources and a lot of insight. I also owe a lot to my city of Nashville, which served as a backdrop and key character for several stories of civics education renewal. I am also forever grateful for the advice and encouragement of friends and amazing writers Annie Murphy Paul, Jessica Lahey, Devorah Heitner, and Stephen Ornes. They generously shared their knowledge with me and illuminated the path of how to go about writing a book. And I thank the nearly 50 generous, wonderful teen activists who shared their stories with me and taught me all about how our democracy looks through their eyes.

Finally, I'm grateful that I got to learn more about civics through this process. I realized in the writing of this book that I am incredibly grateful to the United States of America and the promise of America, as imperfect as she is, and the American style of democracy—a democratic republic or a constitutional democracy, whichever you prefer—that allowed my life, and the lives of those I love, to flourish. Let's work hard to ensure a future where that kind of freedom and opportunity is available to all.

Introduction

Knowledge about our government is not handed down through the gene pool.
Every generation has to learn it, and we have some work to do.
—Former Supreme Court Justice Sandra Day O'Connor

On the Saturday after the massacre of 17 teenagers at Marjory Stoneman Douglas High School in Parkland, Florida—one of more than 300 mass shootings and 23 school shootings in the United States in 2018—people gathered in front of a federal courthouse in Fort Lauderdale for a rally for gun control. Emma González, a high school senior who survived the shooting, stood up and began to speak to the crowd, her face marked by grief, her voice emotional and raw. And then something remarkable happened: González held up a bunch of crinkled paper, notes from her Advanced Placement (AP) Government class, and began to read aloud from them, laying out an emotional but articulate case for students and parents to take public action in order to prevent more school shootings. "If all our government can do is send thoughts and prayers," she practically yelled through tears, "then it's time for victims to be the change we seek."

González's speech soon became a catalyst for youth activism in the weeks that followed. González and fellow Parkland students David Hogg, Cameron Kasky, Jaclyn Corin, and others quickly rallied a nationwide student movement reminiscent of the first teens to engage in the civil rights protests of the 1960s. They organized a nationwide student walk-out to protest gun violence, and an estimated one million students from Boston, Massachusetts, to Boise, Idaho, walked out of their schools. Parkland students descended on Washington, DC, for the March for Our Lives, reportedly one of the biggest protests ever to take place in the capital and with an estimated 200,000 people—adults and youth—attending, which inspired more than 800 sister protests around the country and the world.

Around the same time, Parkland teen Kyle Kashuv was also at work, rallying pro–Second Amendment students and beginning work on an app to help kids find emotional support, which he said was sorely lacking at school. His advocacy was so thoroughly convincing, he earned an invitation to the White House. Though they represented different viewpoints on how to deal with school gun violence, the Parkland teens' ability to advocate for their cause held every American's attention. Adults were stunned, and young people inspired. Common media portrayals of young people as navel-gazing and apathetic melted away as more grownups started asking: what's so different about these teenagers? How did they break through the noise of an extremely polarized country?

The Parkland teens' activism was no accident. They had been in middle school when Florida had decided to ramp up civics education in school, and passed a law requiring all middle schoolers to take a full year of civics to study legislative procedures and debate controversial issues. As seventh graders after the law was passed, González and Hogg had been part of the very first class. While it may not seem significant, or even necessarily the cause for their advocacy, national data show that the kind of robust civics education these students received in middle school is not common. Once at the heart of American schooling, over the last 50 years civics—the study of learning how to be a citizen—has largely declined in public schools.

Civics is the study of the three branches of government and how the Electoral College works, but it's also learning about the foundations and values our democratic republic was built on, such as equality and individual rights. Civics is also learning about how to participate as a citizen—voting, volunteering, serving on juries, and working with government and elected officials to solve challenges. Civics education prepares young people for all aspects of public life, not just political life—learning how to be a positive part of a community, respect differences, care for the welfare of others, and pay attention to current events.

Civics education was the purpose for creating the American public school system; founding fathers like Thomas Jefferson emphasized the importance of raising knowledgeable citizens in order for the country to stay free. "The qualifications for self-government in society are not innate. They are the result of habit and long training," Jefferson wrote, along with "[Without becoming] familiarized with the habits and practice of self-government . . . the political vessel is all sail and no ballast."[1]

But over the last 50 or 60 years, for a variety of reasons we'll discover in later chapters, schools have stopped teaching civic knowledge. States don't test it, and some don't even require a civics or government class before high school graduation. In 2015 the Thomas B. Fordham Institute reviewed the mission and values statements of the 100 largest school districts in the country and found that teaching citizenship didn't appear to be a top priority.

While many districts mentioned "college and career" as a goal, 60 percent of districts didn't mention "civics, citizenship, or democracy" at all.[2]

Not teaching civics means that most young people graduating from high school don't know how the government works or the rights and responsibilities of citizens, and scholars have connected the decline in civics education to the decline in the general population's civic knowledge. In a nationwide evaluation of what students know about civics, the National Assessment of Educational Progress (NAEP), also called the "Nation's Report Card," found that only one-quarter of eighth graders knew enough to score "proficient" or higher on the civics exam. For U.S. history, only 18 percent scored above "proficient."[3] Lack of knowledge shows up in adulthood, too: shockingly, a 2017 poll by the Annenberg Public Policy Center found that nearly 40 percent of Americans couldn't name a single right provided by the First Amendment to the Constitution. Only one in four Americans were able to name all three branches of government, and one-third couldn't name a single branch.[4]

When people don't know anything about how government works, then it becomes increasingly difficult for them to be engaged with it. It's no surprise, then, that as civics education disappeared, a sharp increase in civic challenges have appeared in its place. A giant chasm has split open between our constitutional republic and us—the people it is intended to serve. America is facing civic problems such as record-low voter participation, high rates of political polarization, and high levels of skepticism and cynicism about our government. As experts David E. Campbell, Meira Levinson, and Frederick M. Hess wrote in their 2012 book *Making Civics Count*, "By nearly every measure, Americans are less engaged in their communities and political activity than in generations past."[5]

The United States now holds one of the lowest voter participation rates among developed countries, according to the Pew Research Center, which has extensively researched the changing politics and civic engagement of Americans. In 2016, only 55.7 percent of the voting-age population went to the polls, while in the United Kingdom 63 percent voted, and in South Korea, 77.9 percent. Among Americans ages 18 to 24, the rate is even lower—20 percent.[6] If young people aren't excited about voting, it may be because they do not trust that their vote makes much of a difference. Public trust has eroded, and the vast majority of Americans in 2017—82 percent—say they do not trust the government to do what's right or in people's best interest.[7] As of December 2018, the public's approval of the job Congress was doing was an abysmal 18 percent.[8]

The inability of Congress to do what constituents want might be caused and exacerbated in part by a growing partisan ideological divide between Democrats and Republicans, a divide that is becoming increasingly more toxic and rendering policy-making nearly impossible. This divide is happening in the public, too, as political polarization divides neighborhoods and families and is getting darker—partisans are seeing the opposition not just as a difference in opinion, but a "danger to the republic." In a survey from *Public Opinion Quarterly* back in 1960, participants were asked whether they'd be upset if their child married outside their family's political party; 5 percent of Republicans and 4 percent of Democrats admitted they'd be unhappy. In 2010, that number jumped to 49 percent and 33 percent, respectively.[9] The effects of polarization even reached the Oval Office. In January 2016, in his final State of the Union address, a graying and embattled President Obama made a plea to Congress to reform polarized politics that morphed into a plea to reform polarized America. "Democracy does require basic bonds of trust between citizens," he said.

But experts worry the basic bonds of trust might be fraying for a system in decline. Political researchers Roberto Stefan Foa and Yashca Mounk found that support for democracy as a political system had diminished significantly in the last two decades. Drawing on data gathered from the World Values Survey, in which social scientists around the globe measure how changing values impact society, Foa and Mounk found that American citizens (along with some of their Western European counterparts) had not only become more critical of their political leaders, but more "cynical about the value of democracy as a political system, less hopeful that anything they might do might influence public policy, and more willing to express support for authoritarian alternatives." They called this a "crisis of legitimacy" that was much bigger than they expected.[10]

Survey data showed that overall, democracy and democratic ideals held less value than they did a few decades ago (figure 0.1). For example, interest in politics declined over the last few decades—in 1990, 53 percent of young Americans ages 16 to 35 were interested in politics, but by 2010, that number had dropped 12 points, to 42 percent. In 2010, only 32 percent of young American millennials (ages 22 to 37) reported that it was "absolutely essential" in a democracy that "civil rights protect people's liberty." And 26 percent said that free elections are unimportant in a democracy. Astonishingly, when looking over the last three decades of survey data, Americans seem more friendly now to the idea of military rule: though only 1 in 16, or 6 percent, were in favor of army rule in 1990, that number is 1 in 6 (16 percent) today.[11]

HOW CIVICS EDUCATION DISAPPEARED

How did interest in civics disappear? As a journalist covering the decline of civics in schools, I started to wonder how important civics education was to students and teachers. I wanted to know exactly why civics had declined, and

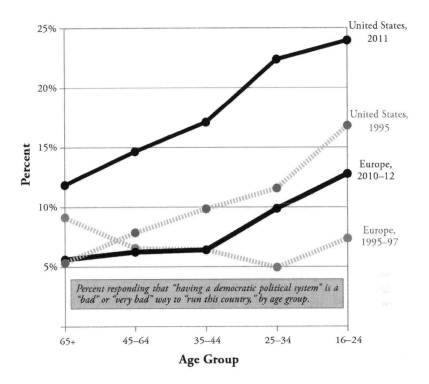

Figure 0.1.   Having a Democratic Political System Is a "Bad" or "Very Bad" Way to Run This Country. *Published with permission. Figure originally appeared in the July 2016 issue of* Journal of Democracy.

whether anyone had noticed. And, most importantly, I wanted to know where bright spots existed.

When I started looking into it, I found that inside America lies a kind of civics cognitive dissonance: while many young Americans were pulling away from public life, questioning politics, and even the idea of democracy itself, young people like Emma, David, Cameron—and, I was about to find out, many more—were jumping *into* public life. And they were doing it waving their AP Government notes in their hands. Behind these two polar pieces of information is a bigger story, one about how young people learn, or don't learn, how to be citizens.

Through a year of research, I combed through data, visited schools, and interviewed teachers. I spoke to parents to find out if they knew whether their children received civics instruction at school, and experts who had been studying civic health for decades. I looked into religious settings, youth groups, after-school clubs, and community organizations. And I found that the decline of civics was not new, but had been decades in the making.

As the world became more globalized, many thought that old-fashioned civics was no longer needed. In the 1990s a political scientist had even predicted that modern, Western-style liberal democracy would be the "final form of human government."[12] After reports such as the 1983 *A Nation at Risk: The Imperative for Educational Reform* and legislation like the 2001 No Child Left Behind Act emphasized gaps in student achievement, over time schools modified their missions from civic purpose to preparing kids for college and career. Then, under extreme pressure, districts became focused (some would say obsessed) with raising standardized test scores in reading and math, which didn't leave much time for learning "extras" like history and the workings of government. The culture at large moved away from civics, too—the institutions that supported young people, across the board, took on more pressing concerns.

But I found that the impact of the loss of civics has been considerable in schools. Many teachers voiced worries: the United States of America feels like it's on the edge of a dangerous precipice, some told me. Political, economic, and racial divides are deepening, enflamed by social media posts and false and misleading "news" articles able to spread misinformation like wildfire. Some teachers spoke about the way kids relate to each other feeling fundamentally broken.

Like-minded tribes on social media and in the community entrench beliefs with groupthink, making it harder to bridge political and cultural divides. Holly Kartchner, a government teacher in Blackfoot, Idaho, described how after the 2016 presidential election, some students at her school chased and harassed Latino and immigrant students, yelled at them to "go back where they came from." Meg Hopkins, a fourth-grade teacher in Vermont, said many families in her school were being affected by the opioid crisis, and some of her students were left without a community they could rely on. Amanda Smithfield, a high school librarian in Nashville, Tennessee, worried that the minority of conservative students in her left-leaning high school didn't feel comfortable expressing their opinions in class. Jose Flores, a government teacher in Brawley, California, said his students from immigrant families felt they didn't have a voice or an opinion in their community.

But had anyone besides educators seemed to care? Yes, they had been concerned—for years. Experts and grassroots organizations in civics had been sounding the alarm for two decades about what might happen if young people didn't learn civics. Back in 2003, way before "tribal politics" or "fake news" had appeared on the scene, the Carnegie Corporation of New York and the Center for Information and Research on Civic Learning and Engagement (CIRCLE) issued the *Civic Mission of Schools* report, which detailed the way a lack of civics education could affect our democracy for generations to come. As a way to reach as many students as possible, former Supreme Court Justice Sandra Day O'Connor launched a free online game called iCivics in 2009 to present real-life civic problems for students so they could better understand the government.

So efforts were being made. But it wasn't until the divisive 2016 election that civics education reached a tipping point, and began to stage a comeback. Not all at once, but in pockets, groups of dedicated teachers, schools, grassroots groups, and even some statehouses, alarmed by what they have seen in public life, have been energized into action and are working to put civics education back into young people's lives. The revival is not just happening in classrooms, but in gymnasiums, after-school programs, clubs, and houses of worship. It's even happening in living rooms between parents.

"For a variety of reasons, the election of 2016 was the culminating moment," said Ted McConnell, director of the Campaign for the Civic Mission of Schools. McConnell has been working to spread the gospel of civics education for more than 20 years, but said in an interview it was only when civic challenges became very clear that anyone started listening. "Though our work hasn't changed, what's changed is the amount of attention we're getting. I think people have finally realized that we have incredible divisions in our country, and that's grabbed people. We've got to do better—this is important to the future of our Republic."

But in the 50 years since civics mattered, a lot has changed—the world has changed, the economy has changed and, perhaps most of all, the young American herself has changed. Globalization, incredible advances in technology, and new ways of educating and parenting mean that in order to reach students, civics education needed a makeover. So if you're imagining this book as a kind of flag-waving patriotic activity reminiscent of the Fourth of July parades in your grandmother's hometown, it's time to expand your lens. The civics education making a comeback in today's schools is designed specifically for the twenty-first-century kid—the digitally connected, savvy kid who has never known life without the internet and can't imagine a life without his phone. The kid whose own gene pool is a melting pot: multiracial and multicultural by birth. The kid who gets her news, if she reads any at all, from Facebook and Twitter. The kid who most likely lives in a neighborhood where politically, everyone thinks just like her and her family. The kid who may not even know another kid who doesn't believe the way she does. This new kind of kid needs a new civics.

For this twenty-first-century citizen, the new civics doesn't cover just history and government—though these are still the bedrock foundation of any civics education—but has expanded to include media literacy, to help students analyze and evaluate what they read online for truth and facts; a rebranded revival of character education, to solidify what it means to be an upstanding member of a community; community-building, to give alienated and disenfranchised young people a sense of community; lessons in civil discourse, to get young people listening and talking to people with diverse points of view; and perhaps most importantly, action civics, which takes students out of the textbook and into the community by asking young people to identify a problem facing their community and collaborate to take civic action to try and solve it.

Around the country, the new civics is taking shape. In New York City, a small organization called Civic Spirit has been called to bring civics back to religious schools, showing teachers and school leaders how to tie being a good citizen to faithfulness. Meg Hopkins in Vermont incorporated elements of place-based education to help ground her students affected by addiction within a community that helps them feel a sense of belonging. Amanda Smithfield's high school library has become ground zero of openness to diverse viewpoints. She started Project Civility, where students of differing political viewpoints get together once a month and discuss a current events issue over lunch while practicing listening, responding with civility, and giving fact-based answers. In California, Jose Flores is getting his government students out of the classroom to solve environmental issues in their agricultural community, providing them with the tools to find the voice they believe is missing.

The new civics is also showing up at the district and state level. A new civics law in Massachusetts recommends not only beefing up history and civics standards, but also includes funding for project-based civics that gets students working on local problems and being active parts of democracy. And the 2011 Florida law to improve civics mandates a year-long civics course in middle school and debate courses through middle and high school.

But will the new civics "work"? Like so many ideas in education, the honest answer is: it's complicated. And as with any education-based initiative, the road back to educating for citizenship is long and won't be easy— schools are already trying to do so much. Too often, students who receive the most civics in school—wealthier, whiter students—live in communities where civics is built in. The schools needing civics education the most—low-income schools—are the schools that, in many cases, can least afford to offer it.

To change this dynamic, civics experts say the most reliable path to success combines the grassroots efforts and advocacy of parents, educators, and civic groups on the ground while influencing state policy at the top. Changing how a large, diverse country thinks about educating citizens takes sustained energy that lasts long past the tumultuous times we find ourselves in now. Bringing civics back also requires a mind shift to what's important— though civics doesn't have the blockbuster appeal of rolling out a shiny new STEM (science, technology, engineering, and mathematics) lab or football stadium, it is critically important for all young people, and worth fighting for.

The civics education revival happening right now in schools, churches and synagogues, community centers, and streets across the country provides an opportunity to harness and expand the energy already in motion. Energy from the new civics influenced the 2018 midterm elections, which saw the highest youth participation since researchers began collecting data in 1994.[13] The new civics has the potential not only to bring more Americans back into political and civic involvement, but also to combat polarization and rebuild a stronger and more resilient democracy. But to do that, young people from all walks of life will need to be taught a high-quality civics education, and schools should not bear all the responsibility. Civics can be taught, and should be taught, in homes and community organizations and houses of worship, too.

This book is the story of what happens when young people have the opportunity to learn about how to be a citizen in a democracy, and how to be a good citizen at home, with their friends and family, in their schools, and out in the world. Since there was no way I could possibly cover every aspect of civics education—it's a wide topic that covers everything from learning the rules in kindergarten to a senior year government class to a whole lot in between—I chose to focus on the aspects that are changing because of the particular time and place in which we find ourselves now, in the first decades of the twenty-first century, and the particular challenges we face in the United States.

On the day she made her historic speech, Emma González didn't wave her wrinkled AP Government notes by accident—she had practiced debating the issue of gun control in class only days before. It turns out that González, along with her classmates, was receiving one of the best civics educations in the country. She had already learned how to make change in her community. And she brought her notes.

Chapter One

The Rise of the Twenty-First-Century Citizen

For Today's Young People, a New Civics

Civics education matters for this simple reason: It is difficult to expect people to value or participate in what they do not know.

—Anne Wicks

Tuhin Chakraborty was the Quiz Bowl champion of Troy High School, a trivia buff living in leafy Troy, Michigan, a suburb of Detroit. Tuhin played Quiz Bowl, which is a lot like the TV trivia game Jeopardy, in an after-school club and was the team's resident expert on political, American, and European history. His five-person team made it to the Quiz Bowl national competition four times. Tuhin loved Quiz Bowl so much, he started an after-school group that focused on history trivia, just for fun. When he was club president in his senior year, he'd invite students to his house in the evenings to practice—they'd spend an entire night over pizza and his mother's home-made cookies asking questions about not just history, but literature, science, and art as well.

Tuhin loved learning and was an excellent student, but at the same time felt restless and unfulfilled. A self-described "hands-on" learner, he searched for a way to apply all that he knew about politics and history. He thought about great figures through history, all the cool things people had done to change the course of events. He didn't want to just be the passive bystander who learned about historic figures—he wanted to be one.

In the spring semester of 2017 of his junior year, Tuhin was taking AP U.S. Government with Mr. Werenka, a teacher who Tuhin said saw his ambition to move on from knowing to doing. The 2016 presidential election

1

was still a topic that was front and center in class that spring semester, and often Mr. Werenka would lead discussions about the twists and turns of the difficult, highly polarizing election (Tuhin's private nickname for the class was "AP Trump"). In February, Mr. Werenka told Tuhin about an opportunity for high school students to get involved in politics, a fellowship for students just like Tuhin. Mr. Werenka encouraged him to apply, and to Tuhin's surprise, he got it. He was one of 25 high schoolers across the country chosen to attend a series of events put on by a nonprofit organization, Citizen University, in order to "empower and connect a rising generation of civic leaders and doers."

Tuhin flew to Seattle, excited but unsure what to expect from the group, called the Youth Collaboratory. On the first night he met Eric Liu, the founder of Citizen University and a former speechwriter and policy adviser for President Bill Clinton, and heard him speak. That night, Tuhin heard something from Liu he'd never considered before in all his learning about American history and politics: the concept of power, who holds power, and how to get more of it.

Liu explained that, to create change, power is the key—not good or bad in itself, it depends on how you use it—but it's absolutely necessary for understanding politics and civic life. As Liu wrote in his book on grassroots political movements, *You're More Powerful Than You Think*: "Citizens in fact can create power out of thin air—without taking it from anyone else—and often do. There is no limit to the amount of power in a polity. Power is positive-sum, not zero-sum. . . . Power is what we allow it to be. If we remember the limited reserves of power within each of us—and within us collectively—then we can change the math of power. Smalls can become equal to, or greater than, the large."[1]

Power, Liu told the teenagers that night, made political change, and everyday citizens have power—they just need to learn how to use it. Tuhin had thought that in order to create political change, he would need the charisma of Luke Skywalker or the bully pulpit of the president. But Liu called attention to how, in a democracy, the power belonged to the people; all people had to do was realize this and act on it.

Tuhin returned home from the Youth Collaboratory with new ideas and a new sense of urgency. As soon as he got back to Troy, he signed on to work for a political campaign, a national congressional primary race in his district. Tuhin began working after school for the campaign, both as a finance intern and neighborhood canvasser. After several months of hard work after school and on weekends, his candidate won the primary, and Tuhin was elated. He felt a sense of overwhelming accomplishment and vindication that Liu had been right—he *did* have more power than he thought.

After the school year ended, that summer Tuhin connected online with a few friends from the Collaboratory, including Olivia Wu from California,

Alan Cruz from Nevada, and two others to hash out ideas for another civics project. They came up with a website and blog for other young people like them looking to make change. Their collaboration resulted in Ground ONE (for Organize, Network, and Engage), an online gathering place for teenagers who want to get political, with blog posts about issues important to teens across the political spectrum as well as toolkits for activism. In the first months that Ground ONE went live, the students received more than 160 member applications from not only the United States but all over the world— teens from Kosovo, Spain, Turkey, China, India, and others signed up for the toolkits and submitted blog posts about political issues they were dealing with in their countries.

For Tuhin, Mr. Werenka and the Youth Collaboratory changed everything. In all the years he'd been in school, Tuhin felt directed to focus on STEM subjects, but he believed school should focus more on how to be a citizen.

THE TWENTY-FIRST-CENTURY YOUNG AMERICAN

Like many of today's young citizens, Tuhin is coming of age in a moment of particular tumult as a result of profound technological, cultural, economic, and political changes, and his choice to get involved politically in many ways springs from that environment. In order to better understand the new civics education being revived in schools, it's helpful to first understand what kind of citizens need to be educated. These young citizens tend to have several characteristics in common: born at or after the turn of the century, culturally and racially diverse, digitally connected at all times, deeply aware of social problems, and often raised with overprotective parenting practices. Better understanding some of these common characteristics will reveal a bit of who they will be as older citizens, as well as how to provide a civics education that meets their needs in this unique time in history.

Generation Z Is the Most Racially and Culturally Diverse In History, and the Best Educated

The young people of Generation Z,[2] born anywhere between 1997 to the early 2000s, are also called the "pluralist generation." Impacted by a late-twentieth-century influx of non-European immigrants from South and Central America, Southeast Asia, and Africa,[3] the first children of the new century and new millennium are the most racially and culturally diverse in U.S. history, with nearly half being racial or ethnic minorities (figure 1.1).[4] In addition, census numbers reveal that those identifying as mixed race exploded between 2000 and 2010. Members of Generation Z also report a more diverse social circle, and are more likely than their parents or grandparents to say they have friends and acquaintances who are mixed race, African American, Hispanic, Muslim, and Evangelical Christians. [5]

Generation Z is also on track to be the most educated generation in history, with nearly 60 percent of 18 to 20 year olds in college, compared to millennials at 53 percent college attendance and Generation X at 43 percent. Almost half of Generation Z lives with at least one parent with a college degree.

Though the oldest members of Generation Z are entering college, experts trying to predict how increased racial diversity and greater education attainment will affect their lives suggest that their ideas about equality will be vastly different from those of previous generations.

Generation Z Is Digitally Connected and Has Never Known Any Other Way

Generation Z has never known a time without the internet, and nearly all of the 11 million of them—95 percent—has a smartphone. [6] They are "digital natives" who self-report that they are almost always online, continuously digitally connected—some might even say addicted. Media groups who study consumer habits say that today's teenagers have an online attention span of about 8 seconds before they get bored; nearly half of teens report spending *10 hours a day* online. All that time on the internet is mostly spent on social media such as YouTube, Instagram, and Twitter. [7]

Is their internet indulgence a good thing or a bad thing? That depends, and the research in the new field of young people, technology, and well-being is mixed. Psychologist Jean Twenge's research on the phone habits of Generation Z (she calls them iGen) paints a complex picture: spending much of their time in their bedrooms with their phone, today's teenagers are physically safer than they've ever been. They are also much less likely to try alcohol and drugs than their parents. But in her book *iGen: Why Today's Super-Connected Kids Are Growing Up Less Rebellious, More Tolerant, Less Happy*, Twenge looks at the connection between near-constant smartphone usage, especially social media, and rapid rises of youth anxiety and depression. [8]

Twenge's research shows that today's teens differ largely from past generations, even from the millennials who came right before them. Today's teens are growing up more slowly, and more anxious and depressed. In 2016 nearly 20 percent of girls reported a serious depressive episode, up from just 11 percent just 10 years before. Rates of teen suicide have also shot up; according to the Centers for Disease Control, the number of teens committing suicide has increased by more than 70 percent since 2006. In 2016, 5 out of every 100,000 white teens committed suicide; for black teens, it was

Nearly half of post-Millennials are racial or ethnic minorities

% of 6- to 21-year-olds who are nonwhite

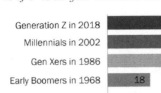

Generation Z in 2018   48%
Millennials in 2002   39
Gen Xers in 1986   30
Early Boomers in 1968   18

More post-Millennials pursuing college

Among 18- to 20-year-olds who are no longer in high school, % enrolled in college

Generation Z in 2017   59%
Millennials in 2002   53
Gen Xers in 1986   44
Early Boomers in 1968   N/A

Post-Millennials more likely than Millennials to live with a college-educated parent

% of 6- to 17-year-olds living with a parent who has at least a bachelor's degree

Generation Z in 2018   43%
Millennials in 2002   32
Gen Xers in 1986   23
Early Boomers in 1968   16

Note: Nonwhites include blacks, Hispanics, other races and people who identify with more than one race.
Source: Pew Research Center analysis of 1968, 1986, 2002 and 2018 Current Population Survey Annual Social and Economic Supplement (IPUMS) and 1986, 2002 and 2017 Current Population Survey October Supplement (IPUMS). "Early Benchmarks Show Post-Millennials on Track to Be Most Diverse, Best-Educated Generation Yet"

PEW RESEARCH CENTER

Figure 1.1.   Nearly half of post-millennials are racial or ethnic minorities. *Pew Research Center, November 13, 2018.*

nearly 3 out of every 100,000, an increase of 77 percent in the previous 10 years.[9]

Yet teens themselves report that social media can also have a positive impact on their lives. In a Pew Research poll in 2018, 31 percent of teens reported that social media has an overall "positive effect" on their lives, allowing them to connect with family and friends. Forty-five percent said that the effect of Snapchat and Twitter was neutral, neither positive nor negative.[10] In late 2018, two researchers looked at data for about 350,000 adolescents and found that although there was no significant correlation between digital technology use and well-being, they noted that previous research (like Twenge's) leaned on weak correlations that might have led to the wrong conclusions.[11]

When it comes to civics, for kids like the activists in Parkland and Tuhin in Michigan, social media was a key tool in spreading their political messages. Social media is also a tool to encourage others to join a cause. For Tuhin, the internet allowed him to connect with others around the world who had a similar passion for getting involved in politics. Without it, there would be no Ground ONE.

Generation Z Has Been Shaped By Overprotective Parenting and Polarized Politics

In their 2018 book, *The Coddling of the American Mind*, psychologist Jonathan Haidt and attorney Greg Lukianoff examined the cultural phenomenon of "safe spaces," "trigger warnings," and the all-or-nothing identity politics that came about almost overnight with the arrival of Generation Z on college campuses in the middle of the 2010s. Though many complex factors converged to create this phenomenon, and the authors avoid simple explanations, one argument Haidt and Lukianoff make concerns growing up in a culture of parent anxiety that has shaped young people's outlook on life and how people treat them. They describe a modern culture of parental "safetyism" and overprotection that both wants to see their children succeed at the highest levels and also sees potential danger on every corner, a style of raising kids they dub "paranoid parenting." While "paranoid parenting" particularly affects middle-class and upper-middle-class children, the authors note many working-class and poor children have been affected by receiving *too little* attention from overworked caregivers and were exposed to *too much* stress, also damaging development and making young college students more afraid.[12]

At the same time, today's teens and young adults have come of age at a time of distressingly high political polarization after a long period of relative centrism and agreement between parties. As journalist Bill Bishop explains in his book *The Big Sort*, cultural, political, and economic forces have caused families over the past few decades to self-segregate into like-minded communities, meaning that many of today's young people have grown up without knowing many people (or sometimes any people) who disagree with them or their family on issues like gun control, health care, or climate change. [13]

Both self-sorting and the "culture of safetyism," when taken to extremes, can affect young people's outlook on civic participation and put strains on democracy by limiting access to a diversity of ideas and speech.

Generation Z Cares about Social Issues and Wants to Make a Difference

Statistics about safe spaces, suicide, and depression might lead you to believe that Generation Z is more self-absorbed than previous generations, but early research shows a more complex picture. Growing up in an age of intractable, "wicked" social problems [14] such as climate change, terrorism, gun violence, and income inequality, and having those social problems constantly reinforced by the news and social media apps on their smartphones, may have made Generation Z *more* aware of their civic responsibility to find solutions, not less.

Early research into these very young Americans shows that 84 percent of teens "support equality for all people," and 88 percent of young people ages 18 to 24 want to live in a "community with high levels of volunteer and community activism." [15] This is already true for millennials, who have shown that they care a great deal about corporate social responsibility and also have high rates of volunteerism—one 2016 poll found that 46 percent of millennials had volunteered their time, and 52 percent had donated money to causes they cared about in the previous month. [16]

These generalizations only form a snapshot of the generation of young people coming up, not a complete picture, but the trends are instructive. When thinking about how to reimagine civics education for the twenty-first century, it's important to consider young people who are the most ethnically and culturally diverse in history, attached to their smartphones, raised in polarized enclaves in childhoods that provided either too much or too little protection from harm, and knowledgeable about social issues and having a desire to make change. In thinking about how to raise these youth for public life, there's no doubt that their needs will be different from the civic needs of the latchkey, "slacker" Generation Xers or the glass-half-full baby boomers, who came of age after World War II.

In many ways, Tuhin embodies the young citizen of the "pluralist" generation. Born at the top of the new millennium and the new century, he has never lived a day without the powerful presence of the internet to order his clothes, connect with his friends, and learn unlimited amounts of the history trivia that he loves. He's also a second-generation American, like 20 million others,[17] born in the Midwest but straddling two identities—Indian and American. His father arrived from an impoverished Calcutta neighborhood in 1981, and his mother followed in 1998. Troy, Michigan, is close to his father's job as an engineer at Chrysler and his mother's as a health care aid in an elementary school; Troy also has a large Indian community that makes up more than 5 percent of the population.

Yet Tuhin calls his life typically American: his father embraces his Americanness, speaking English and having American friends, while his mother works to cultivate their Indian roots, having many Indian friends. Tuhin grew up speaking both Bengali and English at home, but his younger brother, born only five years after him, knows limited Bengali and speaks only English. Like so many Americans, the Chakrabortys are a melting pot within a melting pot.

Tuhin has often said that he wants more than to merely know things; he wants to *do* things—create things, like his group's political activism website, Ground ONE. He also wanted to collaborate with other teenagers and share ideas, whether in person or through social media or video chat. And even though he loved facts, more than once he has referred to himself as a "hands-on" learner—a reference to a debunked education philosophy that posits different kids have optimum "learning styles."

But the hands-on learning Tuhin refers to has its roots in another set of new ideas about how to educate kids in a society that's rapidly evolving, ideas that have emerged in the last 20 years, based largely on the thinking and research of a former high school English teacher named Tony Wagner. According to Wagner, today's students will need a radically different set of skills to succeed in this globalized, interconnected world of constant change—the same skills that young citizens will need to participate in democracy.

HOW "TWENTY-FIRST-CENTURY SKILLS" IMPACT CIVICS

Wagner has been involved in education his entire career, first as a classroom teacher and later earning graduate degrees from Harvard, and being both the Expert in Residence at the Harvard Innovation Lab and directing the Change Leadership Group at the Harvard Graduate School of Education. In 2005 Wagner read a book by Thomas Friedman, *The World Is Flat*, that changed his perspective on education. In the book Friedman explained that because of the internet, the whole world had been transformed, connected in a way that it's never been before. That connectivity changed everything—from the economy, to global security and foreign policy, to education. Wagner has written that the book also changed him—an "incredible eye-opener"[18] that caused him to look at the newly flat world through the lens of education:

were schools preparing twenty-first-century students for this radically different world? What was needed to succeed in an economy that no longer relied on manual labor or solely knowledge, but on the ability to innovate?

To find out, Wagner began interviewing experts from all backgrounds—CEOs and senior leaders in business and the military—to ask what qualities they were looking for in workers and public servants. He quickly realized that in a world where knowledge was a commodity available 24/7 through the internet, acquiring the most knowledge was no longer the most valued skill. Instead, leaders from all backgrounds told him that they were looking for a set of skills and dispositions that were more social and analytical in nature—skills that ranged from the ability to collaborate well with others, to the ability to access and analyze streams of information, to the ability to think creatively, create new products, and solve problems.

Wagner saw that schools weren't teaching these skills, and in many ways were still focusing too much on basic knowledge acquisition. He analyzed the gaps between what classrooms were offering and what businesses and colleges were looking for, and came up with a list of the "seven survival skills" that young people will need to be successful workers—and citizens—in the twenty-first century.

Tony Wagner's Seven Survival Skills for the Twenty-First Century

1. *Critical thinking and problem solving*, which begins with the ability to formulate the right questions. Young citizens can use this skill for lots of civic purposes, from thinking about whom to vote for to understanding "wicked" social and cultural problems.
2. *Collaboration across networks and leading by influence*, which involves working with teams, either in person or online, with people who are diverse in culture and ethnicity. To spur social and political change, young people need to know how to work with people from different backgrounds, races, and religions.
3. *Agility and adaptability*, which serves young citizens living in a society of rapid change where new challenges appear quickly, and new solutions must also be formulated.
4. *Initiative and entrepreneurship*, which involves keeping an "entrepreneurial spirit" of making and setting new goals in both the public and private sphere.
5. *Effective oral and written communication*, which Wagner calls the number one complaint of college professors who argue that "students can't write because they don't know how to think." Solid communication skills serve democracy by giving young people the ability to express and formulate their ideas as well as persuade others to join their thinking.

6. *Accessing and analyzing information*, which involve knowing how to navigate the mass of available information, and the ability to determine its accuracy. These skills are particularly useful in both understanding history and current events.
7. *Curiosity and imagination*, which are just as important to develop as more analytical skills like reasoning and analysis. Young people can dream up civic and social solutions not yet imagined, and use their curiosity to create a better and stronger America.[19]

The seven survival skills don't apply only to college and career but to public life as well, and each can be taken on its own as the means to help citizens in the twenty-first century. But a closer look at an important example, the concept of "fake news"—inaccurate information purposefully written to confuse and mislead readers about important social and political topics—shows us how the skills can be used to strengthen civic dispositions. Fake news is by all measures an important problem facing Americans: research has shown that before the 2016 election, about one in four Americans visited a fake news website that was almost always found through social media sites like Facebook.[20] In another study, lies from fake news were found to spread farther and faster than the truth,[21] much like the old adage that a lie can "travel halfway around the world before the truth can get its pants on."

Fake news sows distrust in readers, making it harder to trust information received from online sources, information that helps us make important decisions like who to vote for, and why. Learning to distinguish real news from fake news does not depend on a particular knowledge base—though awareness of the problem is certainly part of the solution. But a recent study showed that when it comes to discerning real news from fake, skills may trump background knowledge.

In 2017, researchers Joseph Kahne and Benjamin Bowyer published a study on whether background knowledge would help students recognize inaccurate online information. They randomly exposed groups of young people to posts that were accurate and some that were inaccurate, and found that kids who had more political knowledge were not more likely to identify whether something was accurate or not. If anything, the researchers found, young people with political knowledge were slightly *more* likely to make mistakes, and choose posts that tended to reinforce their prior political beliefs as accurate.[22]

Then Kahne and Bowyers exposed the study group to media literacy education, in which teachers show students how to find reliable information sources and give them tools to help them assess content origins. When retested, students were 26 percent more likely to correctly judge a post as accurate, regardless of their prior background knowledge. Media literacy training is a perfect example of how often skills trump knowledge in the twenty-first century, and it incorporates several of Wagner's survival skills, including critical thinking and analyzing information.

But Wagner said that many schools are still educating kids in the old model, teaching a kind of "passive knowledge" without a cohesive framework to use that knowledge to understand the world, which would explain why so many employers told him that their employees lacked the ability to think critically about problems.

But in my own research and reporting, I found that many students aren't learning the "passive" basic knowledge, either. Solid research has shown that background knowledge in subjects like history, science, and the arts gives the mind sturdy and necessary "mental furniture" to support the more complex skills like creativity and critical thinking; without this support, the brain has nothing with which to critically think.[23] In chapter 4 we will explore how lack of background knowledge in history makes it harder for young people to critically think about complex social and civic issues. Because of the increasing complexity of the world, it's vital to have both knowledge and skills in order to be a good American citizen in 2018.

"For the first time in history, the skills you need for work, continuous learning, and citizenship, they're all the same skills," Wagner said in an interview. "In the past, the skills you needed were much more about compliance, but that's all gone. To address today's challenges, whether at work or in your community, you need to be able to think critically, ask the right questions, and work collaboratively. And you have to think creatively about new solutions. . . . The world no longer cares about what kids know. What the world cares about is what kids *can do* with what they know."

HOW TO RAISE CITIZENS IN THE TWENTY-FIRST CENTURY

For Ted McConnell, director for the Campaign for the Civic Mission of Schools who has been involved in promoting civics education for more than 20 years, the need for a new version—complete with new knowledge and skills for the twenty-first century—has never felt so urgent. Two decades ago, concerns about civics being removed from schools to make more room for reading and math—something I focus on in the next couple of chapters—prompted a group of civics experts and organizations to form the Campaign for the Civic Mission of Schools to raise awareness of the need to keep civics a priority. But back in the relative peace and prosperity of the late 1990s, McConnell said, no one was really listening. And it wasn't until the past few years, when stories of intractable political polarization, proliferation of "fake news" shared on social media, the rise of uncivil discourse, and democratic unrest mixed with deeply imbedded social problems of race, inequality, and

immigration surfaced, that people both inside and outside the school community began to wake up and listen to the Campaign's message.

And even though the challenges are relatively new, the goals for civics
education first set forth by the Campaign have stayed the same. In a 2003
report, the Campaign outlines what a citizen should *know* and be able *to do*:
first and foremost, being informed and thoughtful as well as having a "grasp
and an appreciation of history and the fundamental processes of American
democracy." Young citizens should also have the ability to talk to those with
different perspectives, and participate in their communities through social,
cultural, political, and religious organizations. Citizens should have the
"skills, knowledge and commitment" to be able to act politically for public
purpose, not just through voting but also "group problem solving, public
speaking, petitioning and protesting." And finally, young citizens should
possess the kind of civic virtue that translates into "concern for the welfare of
others, social responsibility, tolerance and respect, and belief in the capacity
to make a difference."[24]

With these goals in mind, McConnell and the Campaign created a set of
requirements for a civics education backed by research and classroom best
practices that would help to educate the twenty-first-century young citizen.
Called the "six proven practices" (not to be confused with the "seven survival skills"), the list promised to provide a framework for schools and educators to teach young Americans the "knowledge, skills and dispositions" to
engage in modern American public life.

The six proven practices, which originally appeared in the follow up to
the Civic Mission of Schools report titled *Guardian of Democracy: The Civic
Mission of Schools*,[25] are:

1. *Classroom instruction.* Civic learning begins with instruction in history, civics, government, and other subjects falling under social studies.
   Though class time spent on these subjects is by far the most common
   practice of the six, the report cautions that too little time is devoted to
   civics and social studies in the early grades (a topic visited in chapter
   4), and that teaching should be engaging and interesting, rather than
   "rote facts about dry procedures," which may end up doing more harm
   than good.
2. *Discussion of current events and controversial issues.* Research has
   shown that young people who engage in thoughtful discussion and
   debate of current issues in school tend to have "greater interest in
   politics, improved critical thinking and communication skills, more
   civic knowledge and more interest in discussion of public affairs out
   of school." Learning how to discuss hot-button controversial issues
   has special importance now (discussed in chapter 12), as American
   civil discourse has degenerated.

3. *Service learning.* Students who participate in high-quality service-learning projects, in which students take what they've learned in classrooms, apply it to solve problems and volunteer in their communities (discussed in chapter 13), and show greater interest in civic participation as well as higher academic achievement. Projects in which students have a choice and a voice are more closely linked with increased civic engagement later on.

4. *Extracurricular activities.* Research has shown that students who participate in a wide variety of extracurricular activities, including civic-minded activities like debate team and student council but also performing arts and sports, stay civically engaged throughout their lives. Activities that require collaboration and teamwork show civic benefits, and build the essential "relationship between citizen and society."

5. *Student participation in school governance.* The practice of self-government can begin years before students are of voting age by allowing students a voice and role in the governing of their school community. Research links participation in school governance with building civic skills, and students who participate in activities like student council have been shown to be more likely to vote.

6. *Simulations of the democratic process and "adult" civic roles.* Simulations of civic and political processes, when performed inside school, can have civic benefits by allowing students to "act in fictional environments in ways that would be impossible for them in the real world." Mock trials, constitutional conventions and legislative simulations, and even games are linked to increased political knowledge.

However, after a few years, McConnell and the Campaign watched as political life began to change: as political polarization and digital media became more prominent, along with new research on teaching relationship-based skills, the members decided to add more practices to address new civic challenges and research—ones that focused more on twenty-first-century skills. The new "promising practices" the Campaign endorses are central to the new kind of civics—more hands-on, more focused on digital media, and more focused on showing young people not just how the government works, but how to get involved in public life.

New promising practices include *media literacy*, whereby students learn to analyze accurate and inaccurate news articles and advertisements and tools for finding reliable information sources; *action civics*, in which students choose and attempt to solve a community issue by engaging with local leaders and trying to affect policies; *social-emotional learning* that teaches "soft skills" like managing emotions and how to maintain positive relationships; and *school climate reform,* which includes reducing racial disparities in school discipline and promoting restorative justice.

The six proven practices and seven survival skills work together to make a solid base for raising citizens in the new diverse, digitally connected, extremely polarized world in which we now find ourselves—not just inside of schools, but also in the neighborhoods, houses of worship, and extracurricular activities of American young people. These sets of practices and skills overlap in important ways, such as how government background knowledge (one of the six proven practices) is necessary for the critical thinking (one of the seven survival skills) needed to understand whether a new policy in one's community should be given a yes or no vote. Or how a student council program (one of the six proven practices) can give young people the opportunity to think creatively (one of the seven survival skills) about solutions to problems that affect their community.

Put together, the two skill sets form the foundation of this book. Raising today's citizens must address these three critical areas of young peoples' development:

1. *Acquiring a broad, deep knowledge base.* Americans know surprisingly little about the country in which they live and the government that works for them. This critical knowledge about America's foundations and past can help to inform decisions made for the future. But in order to ensure that Americans are more knowledgeable, schools need to work history classes back into elementary school, in addition to offering government and civics courses in middle and high school. Courses need to prioritize history and government knowledge, as well as provide effective simulations, like mock trials and mock legislative sessions, to give students a feel for how government really works.

   Who receives the best history and civics classes is highly unequal, a fact that will be explored, along with efforts by some states to revamp civics and put it back into schools, in chapter 2. Chapter 4 addresses the history knowledge gap, how social studies and history have been diminished primarily due to emphasis on standardized tests in reading and math, and then highlights some effective programs that bring history knowledge to elementary school students and make democracy come alive for high schoolers.

2. *Forging positive relationships with the self and wider world.* Startling statistics reveal that young Americans are surprisingly lonely and many have few connections to their communities, affecting civic participation. As Alexis de Tocqueville noticed nearly two centuries ago on his trip across America, strong relationships and community ties are essential to our flavor of democracy. But research has shown that many young people live in "civic deserts," with little to no opportunity to participate in any kind of public life.

The middle section of the book is dedicated to exploring how different kinds of human connections are vitally important for civic engagement. Chapter 10 explores twenty-first-century character education, and how too much emphasis on performance values has reduced teaching both the civic values of being community minded and the moral values of taking the right action. Chapter 13 looks at how to strengthen community ties and democratic spaces to combat loneliness and apathy, and increase civic health.

3. *Analyzing different views and taking action.* After acquiring a deep knowledge base and building up the self and community, young citizens are ready to learn to tackle more difficult and complex issues that pose a threat to the United States and democracy at large. Chapter 10 takes a look at the first of these threats, what researchers Jennifer Kavanagh and Michael D. Rich call "truth decay"—the "growing disregard for facts, data, and analysis in political and civil discourse in the United States."[26] Media literacy can stop truth decay, and will be explored in detail. Debate team gets remade for the twenty-first century in chapter 12, to explore the future of civil discourse and discussion of controversial issues in a highly polarized society. And chapter 13 looks at the merits and drawbacks of the popular "action civics" programs sweeping the country, in which young people don't just learn about the workings of government but use their knowledge to get hands-on with democracy.

In between chapters are slices of the new civics as it's happening on the ground—mini-biographies of young people and adults who embody the qualities of the twenty-first-century citizen. Some, like Seth Andrew and iCivics, are thought leaders completely reshaping the civics education landscape with their innovative ideas, and some are students participating in the new civics who have been inspired to engage with public life and politics. We'll hear directly from the young citizens themselves, what inspires them, what they wished they knew, and what kind of future they imagine for themselves and their fellow Americans.

But along with the right kind of education and skill-building, students need support to engage in public life. Tuhin's interest in civic and political involvement was no accident—he had lots of help and support along the way. In his high-quality, middle-class school in Troy, Michigan, he learned background information about U.S. history and the political process, piquing his civic interest. He never experienced feeling like an outsider or any overt racism in his community that could have harmed his prospects or discouraged him from entering public life or speaking up; and he had Mr. Werenka, who noticed Tuhin's interest in civics and helped plug him in to the action-based civics project he craved.

He also had support at home—a key ingredient to future civic involvement. As Ted McConnell said, "Parents are a child's first and best civic teachers," and that was true in Tuhin's case. His strong family ties and close relationship with his mother and father increases the chances that he will vote, volunteer, and be civically involved into adulthood, and this is backed by research.[27] When Tuhin became interested in politics in his teen years, his father was an important role model, talking to him from the time he was young about current events as well as what he thought about local and national political candidates.

It appears that making a habit of voting is also influenced by family. In a 2016 article for the *New York Times*, Henry Brady, the dean of the Goldman School of Public Policy at the University of California, Berkeley, said that voting behavior is a habit, and one that is often formed early in life: "If you've had the behavior modeled in your home by your parents consistently voting, by political discussion, sometimes by participation, you start a habit formation and then when you become a little older you'll feel it's your duty and responsibility to register and vote."[28]

Yet many American young people don't have access to the same opportunities as Tuhin—and as a result, many are disconnected from the political process, either by choice or by exclusion, whether purposeful or unconscious. Moreover, many students don't have a solid, high-quality civics program built into their school curriculum or after-school program to make up for what may be lacking at home or in the community. But when supports and opportunities are provided for students—as we will see in the coming chapters—a chance to participate in public life is exciting and life-changing.

"People in high school used to tease me, 'Oh, you're so into politics, why don't you just chill out.'" said Tuhin. But then he said that, after the election of 2016 as the country waded deeper into polarization and hate, after political scandals and indictments roiled the nation, after news that the polar ice caps were melting much faster than expected and waves of gun violence inside schools terrified students and parents alike, something changed. Right before Tuhin's graduation in the spring of 2018, even some of the most apathetic students who knocked him before weren't knocking him anymore.

"Before, they were laughing at me," said Tuhin. "They're not laughing now."

FOR PARENTS AND TEACHERS TO THINK ABOUT

- The young citizens of Generation Z, born at the turn of a new millennium and a new century, are beginning to join civic life. They are the most racially and culturally diverse generation in U.S. history, as well as the best educated; they are connected to their smartphones all the time; they have been shaped by polarized politics and overprotective parenting; and they want to make a difference in society.

- The changes brought about by globalization and technology require a new kind of citizenship and civic participation. Today's young citizens need to be taught a new kind of civics in order to engage with public life, a civics that utilizes technology and the "hands-on" style of a new generation of learners, as well as integrates the "seven survival skills" experts say are necessary for success in the twenty-first century.
- While some aspects of civics education will always remain the same, like the requirement for a deep knowledge base of history and government, some are newer and show promise for addressing current challenges, such as media literacy to combat online misinformation, and action civics.

Chapter Two

Nurseries of a Free Republic

The Critical Role Schools Play in Teaching Citizenship

> I know of no safe depository of the ultimate powers of the society but the people themselves; and if we think them not enlightened enough to exercise their control with a wholesome discretion, the remedy is not to take it from them, but inform their discretion.
>
> —Thomas Jefferson

In 1837, a Massachusetts lawyer and state senator named Horace Mann secured one million public dollars for the creation of a new office that would provide a free education for every child in the state. Like the founding fathers, Mann was driven by an almost religious faith in the power of education to lift anyone out of their circumstances, no matter how bleak, and wanted to make that education available to every American. He also believed that the new immigrants pouring into the nation from a variety of backgrounds and cultures needed a common language in order for American-style representative democracy to work—a kind of civic insurance policy to ensure that every American would understand and appreciate values like equality, liberty, and individual rights.

Mann believed that education would use reading and writing, as well as the study of history and science, to create well-informed citizens and protect against future tyranny—a thought also echoed by the founders. Thomas Jefferson wrote in 1778 that

> the most effectual means of preventing this [tyranny] would be, to illuminate . . . the minds of the people at large, and more especially to give them the knowledge of those facts, which history exhibiteth, that, possessed thereby of the experience of other ages and countries, they may be enabled to know

ambition under all its shapes, and prompt to exert their natural powers to
defeat its purposes. [1]

An educated populace, early Americans wagered, would diminish early
America's concerns of falling for a demagogue or a tyrant.

With the help of local leaders, Mann and the Massachusetts Board of
Education began opening schools in every city, town, and village, and went
on to require all Massachusetts children to attend. These "common schools"
quickly grew in number and spread into the states, igniting a nationwide
public school movement. Soon every state supported a network of locally
run, publicly funded free schools.

But unlike the common school's European counterparts that provided a
liberal arts education rich in intellectual thinking, literature, and the arts—an
education for "private life"—Mann and supporters of "education for the
masses" said the focus of American schools should be to educate young
people for *public* life. As Dana Goldstein writes of Mann in *The Teacher
Wars*, "He considered a French-style liberal arts education irrelevant to the
masses in a popular democracy, where the most important task facing any
man was, as a voter, to assess the moral character of candidates for political
office."[2]

By the mid-nineteenth century, nine out of ten students were enrolled in
public schools, and the curriculum was closely linked to citizenship.[3] Abraham Lincoln even referred to the importance of civics education in one of his
first public speeches at the Young Men's Lyceum in Springfield, Illinois, in
1938:

> Let reverence for the laws, be breathed by every American mother, to the
> lisping babe, that prattles on her lap—let it be taught in schools, in seminaries,
> and in colleges; let it be written in Primers, spelling books, and in Alma-
> nacs;—let it be preached from the pulpit, proclaimed in legislative halls, and
> enforced in courts of justice. And, in short, let it become the political religion
> of the nation.[4]

Mann and his supporters argued that education must help young people
define and understand their role as participating Americans. Therefore, civics
education had to come first: though the fledgling democracy desired scholars, what it needed more was informed citizens.

From the beginning, America placed its hope in schools as the best and
most effective places to grow good citizens—an ideal that endures today,
even when it's not always happening in practice. While most states have
some kind of school civics or government requirement for graduation, critics
claim that one semester, often at the very end of a K–12 school career, isn't
nearly enough to make an impression. Peter Levine, professor of citizenship
and public affairs at Tufts University's Jonathan Tisch College of Civic Life,

writes, "By far the most important providers of civic education are the schools themselves."[5]

Schools are not just the places where students learn civics content and skills—about American government and politics, how to have discussion and debate about important issues, and take leadership roles in student government and after-school clubs—that research shows helps to develop engaged citizens. For many, schools are also the first and most enduring places young people get to experience and practice democratic values such as how to be part of a community, how to collaborate with others, how to work for the common good, how to treat others fairly, and how to interact with honesty and integrity.

The different kinds of civics that have been explicitly taught in schools have changed over time, of course, much of it shaped as a response to social and cultural shifts. During the common school era, civics was more focused on teaching responsibility, morality, and patriotism: schools were outfitted with "McGuffey Readers" that taught reading through stories stressing American "melting pot" values like unity and civic virtue, as well as moral values such as honesty, integrity, and responsibility.[6]

By the early twentieth century, as America absorbed a huge influx of immigrants, industrialization increased, and more students were attending high school than ever before, civics and government was established as its own secondary course separate from U.S. history. In 1916, the National Education Association (NEA) issued the first-ever report on the national state of social studies and recommended that civics instruction be made part of history requirements. Part of the report included recommendations for a ninth-grade course that focused on community civics—"one's place in the local, state and global community"—as well as a "Problems of Democracy" course for seniors.[7]

During this time, interdisciplinary social studies, a relatively new concept, and civics education also became more progressive, mirroring Teddy Roosevelt's Progressive Party reforms that aimed to stop corruption and improve living conditions for factory workers and the poor. In addition, educator and philosopher John Dewey's "community civics" emphasized tolerance and democratic community action at this time, and focused on teaching young people to care for their communities.[8] Rooted in community civics was the idea that democracy was embedded in the schools themselves, and the "people's schools" were democracy in action.

The first half of the twentieth century proved to be civics education's real heyday, where civic participation blossomed both within schools and in the community. Civic-minded, out-of-school community organizations for young people like the Key Club, Boy and Girl Scouts, and 4-H Clubs were founded and flourished during the early parts of the twentieth century. Many sprang up to reinforce "good citizen" character qualities like honesty, integrity, compassion, service to others, and love of community and country. The Scout Oath, published in 1911, blended faith, patriotism, and the concept of the good citizen all together: "On my honor I will do my best to do my duty to God and my country and to obey the Scout Law; to help other people at all times; to keep myself physically strong, mentally awake, and morally straight."[9]

And the pledge of 4-H, a civic club started for farm kids that focused on issues of food and animal husbandry, carried a civic tune: "I pledge my head to clearer thinking, my heart to greater loyalty, my hands to larger service, and my health to better living, for my club, my community, my country."[10]

Public-minded service organizations for adults were also created, and flourished through local chapters during this period: the Rotary Club, Parent-Teacher Associations (PTA), the League of Women Voters, Veterans of Foreign Wars (VFW), the Lions Club, the NAACP, the Knights of Columbus, and Kiwanis, just to name a few.[11] These clubs encouraged civic purpose without being political, and served as models of participation for young people. As French diplomat Alexis de Tocqueville famously noted years before on his trip across the United States, Americans "of all ages, all stations in life, and all types of disposition are forever forming associations."[12]

In many ways, the first half of the twentieth century was an unusually civic-centered age—centrism reigned, polarization was unusually low, and there was high trust in government, perhaps in part because two world wars had united Americans in common purpose.[13] But by the middle of the twentieth century, civics fever had begun to decline as other priorities emerged.

About the time that the United States became more secure in its democracy, the middle class expanded, and living conditions improved, in 1957 the Soviet Union launched the satellite Sputnik into space, prompting the beginning of the "space race." Sputnik sent a shock wave through the education establishment, which feared that Americans weren't learning enough math and science, and schools began to focus more on beefing up STEM programs. Shortly thereafter, the social and cultural upheaval of the 1960s and 1970s cast skepticism and doubt on the authority and institutions the past 50 years of civics education had spent time building, replacing it with a new kind of civic participation—one built on protest. The Vietnam War, campus protests, the civil rights movement, and the women's movement caused profound change in civic participation that included the voices of a much more diverse range of citizens who had previously been marginalized.

Then the standards-based education reform movement of the 1990s cemented into federal law with the No Child Left Behind Act of 2001, altered the direction of what was being taught at school. Strict accountability measures to improve reading and math achievement, demonstrated through the scores of standardized state tests, put pressure on schools to focus attention on reading and math skills, which ended up narrowing curriculum. Under pressure to raise reading and math scores, over the next decade schools began reducing time for social studies (along with other non-reading and non-math subjects like science, music, and art). A 2011 Fordham Institute study showed that between 1987 and 2003, time spent on social studies in elementary school dropped by 18 hours per year.[14] By 2007, the National Center of Education Statistics found that elementary schools spent only about 7 percent of their total instructional hours on social studies.[15] When elementary general education teachers were asked whether subjects like social studies had been crowded out of their curriculum to make room for more reading and math, more than 80 percent of them answered yes.[16]

By the first decades of the twenty-first century, the pursuit of reading and math scores, along with district-wide emphases on STEM subjects, made it clear that raising citizens was no longer the mission of schools. Over the course of a 12- or 13-year school career, the vast majority of today's students—about 90 percent—get about a semester's worth of high school civics or government in order to graduate. Thirty-six states require at least one civics or government course for graduation; eight states require a full year.[17] But the overall civic mission had disappeared—quite literally. As mentioned in the introduction, many of the country's largest school districts no longer even refer to citizenship in their mission statements, instead opting for references to "college and career," "communities of learners," and "global citizenship."[18]

Throughout all the different incarnations of civics education taking place since the establishment of the common schools, one unfortunate fact has remained the same: how unequally civics education has been distributed to students. For nearly all of U.S. history, democratically run schools and civic teaching were largely the privilege of white citizens. Until the late twentieth century Native Americans, African Americans, Latinos, and other minorities were regularly excluded from public education and forced to attend separate schools without adequate funding. Yet even after they were no longer excluded by law from an education, stark inequities in the quality of the education for many children of color still persist.

Entering the twenty-first century, one of civics education's greatest challenges within schools is addressing the inequities that children of color and the poor have endured for centuries. While the American public school was created to give civic knowledge and skills to everyone, equally—"to equalize political power by giving everyone the knowledge and skills they would need to participate," Peter Levine wrote[19]—the education system is still struggling to meet that lofty goal.

ADDRESSING INEQUALITY AND LARGE GAPS IN
CIVIC LEARNING

The first day of senior government class at Community High School in West Chicago, Illinois, begins with an official bang of a gavel. Students spend the first few weeks learning about state issues and figuring out where they stand on these, and make party declarations and hold elections. Then they begin researching and writing bills that will eventually be voted on by the entire senior class.

This isn't a typical senior government class, but an exciting, authentic simulation of a state legislative session with rigorous, parliamentary procedure–style rules that lasts the entire semester—something Community High has been doing since the mid-1990s. A suburban school just west of Chicago, with a racially and economically diverse population, Community High doesn't offer any Advanced Placement or Honors government courses, by design—since its creation more than two decades ago by a social studies teacher, educators have maintained that a class about how democratic government works should include all students, regardless of their test scores or what track they're on.

Candace Fikis has been teaching the Legislative Semester for three years, after a few years teaching a more standard government class at another high school. She's partial to the Legislative Semester, though, saying what makes the class so valuable (as well as popular with students) is the opportunity to research, develop, and then defend ideas on how to make communities better through law. Student representatives from different backgrounds and viewpoints get to argue solutions to prison reform, gun control, tax law, and other issues. And at the end of every semester, just like in statehouses all over the country, the bills with the most support end up getting passed—an invaluable lesson about what it means to be a citizen in a representative democracy.

Fikis said most students treat the issues with great seriousness, as if these were real bills. "There isn't another class in our school that is this hands-on. They become so passionate about it, they get out of committee and they're devoted to getting their bill passed. They are researching in their off-hours; they find experts to back up their claims. And if their bill passes, they are giving each other high-fives. I sometimes have to remind them, 'guys, this is just a simulation.'"

The main reason Community High resisted tracking students by ability in government class, Fikis said, was to try and ease some of the large civic learning gaps that persist between racial and economic groups. Part of closing those gaps comes in the first three years of high school, and Community High has taken steps to beef up history requirements for all students in preparation for Legislative Semester. But Fikis, along with the other educators who use the Legislative Semester simulation, believes the participatory nature of Legislative Semester helps narrow the gaps in civic knowledge that often exist between kids of different races and economic backgrounds.

Research supports the concept; using simulations of adult civic roles is one of the proven best practices from the Civic Mission of Schools, and the Legislative Semester has been named an exemplary curriculum by Illinois's McCormick Foundation.

Gaps in civic learning between different groups of kids show up not just at Community High, but at schools across the country. While educators and experts are well aware that an achievement gap exists in reading and math, they may be less aware of the differences in civic understanding among students from different economic and racial backgrounds. Test scores measuring civic understanding show large gaps in what different groups of students understand about American government.

Recent scores from the national civics exam, the National Assessment of Educational Progress (NAEP; also called the "Nation's Report Card"), show a large gap between white students and their black and Hispanic peers, as well as a gap between upper-income and lower-income students. (There is also overlap between students of color and low-income students as well.) The NAEP test is designed to test students on factual knowledge about the American style of government and foundations of the political system; intellectual skills and how to apply that knowledge, like the ability to analyze or evaluate information; and civic "dispositions" such as understanding a citizen's responsibilities, respecting others, and how to participate.

Results of the NAEP civics exam show concerning gaps in civic knowledge between white and black eighth graders and between white and Hispanic eighth graders. Jon Valant, a Brookings Institute researcher who helped crunch the numbers for a 2017 report on the state of civics education, said the raw NAEP civics scores from 2014 give a fairly accurate picture of what kids know. The mean score was 164 points for white students, and 141 for Hispanic students. For black students, the mean score was 137. "As a rule of thumb, consider that 11 or 12 NAEP test points represent one year of learning," Valant said. "So there is a two-and-a-half year learning gap between what white students know about civics and what black students know."[20] Similar gaps appear between upper- and middle-income kids and their lower-income counterparts: students who qualified for the National School Lunch Program scored 30 points below students who didn't.

Valant said one reason for the yawning racial and economic gaps is that state education policies put the most emphasis on reading and math scores, creating incentives for schools with low test scores—which often include large populations of low-income students and students of color—to put extra resources into raising those scores, often at the expense of teaching other subjects, like social studies.[21]

Meira Levinson defines a good citizen as someone

knowledgeable about politics, history, government, and current events; they need to be skilled communicators, thinkers, deliberators, and actors; they need to be concerned about the common good in addition to their own self-interest, and to believe it is possible and worth trying to make a difference through public action; and they need to become involved in public or community affairs, through some combination of voting, protesting, contacting public officials, mobilizing others, contributing time or money to causes or campaigns, participating in community groups, and other appropriate actions.[22]

For students who don't have access to the knowledge and skills needed to learn how to participate and how to be a good citizen, a second kind of civics gap opens up, one that Levinson has termed the "civic empowerment gap." The civic empowerment gap is a gap in not just civic and political knowledge, but also in skills and power, between white, better-off, well-educated, and native-born citizens and black, low-income, less-well-educated people of color, and naturalized citizens.

Levinson, who is a professor and researcher at the Harvard Graduate School of Education, writes that political influence in America is contained in affluent and middle-class circles; many citizens of color and those who fall on the lowest part of income distribution "speak in a whisper that is lost on the ears of inattentive government."[23] Lack of political influence and participation is often due to lack of political knowledge and skills. She also writes, "It is easy to imagine how people who don't know who their elected representatives are, what the White House's position is on various high-profile policy disputes, or how a bill becomes a law, may find it harder to influence civic life than those who do."[24] Citizens without the civic knowledge and skills they need to participate are much less likely to vote or volunteer.[25] And, as described earlier, lower-income students and students of color are less likely to receive the knowledge and skills they need to participate.

Depriving these students of a robust civics education has had remarkable effects, contributing to low voter turnout and lower civic participation. And in a larger sense, Levinson notes, it weakens democracy, because collective decisions often only reflect the needs and values of those with access to political and community power. To address the civic empowerment gap, Levinson recommends that teachers and schools take steps to give students a chance to practice democratic citizenship: giving students opportunities to talk and listen to one another and practice expressing their opinions, not just in social studies or civics class but throughout the school day; understanding what students know about American history and how their views may be different from an educator's own experiences; develop a school culture and climate that is welcoming and safe, and shows that students matter; giving students a chance to lead through extracurricular activities; and, importantly, allowing students to be part of a classroom or school's governance.

Levinson said in a talk that she finds it extraordinary that schools have students practice writing, reading, and math daily so they may grow up to become readers, writers, and mathematicians, yet when it comes to citizenship—even though every student will grow up to be a citizen—schools spend almost no time having students practice *being a citizen* through opportunities like student leadership and governance.[26]

A CIVICS REVIVAL BREATHES NEW LIFE INTO EDUCATING FOR CITIZENSHIP

Marc Pacheco's constituents don't know what he does in his job as a state senator. The 30-year veteran of the Massachusetts statehouse representing the town of Taunton, 40 miles south of Boston, told the local paper, the *Sun Chronicle*, that in the last few years, calls from constituents who want him to do something about a national issue have increased. Pacheco believes his constituents don't understand the difference between the federal government and the state government.[27]

On the other side of the country, Washington state senator Hans Zeiger is also concerned about what the public knows about how governance works. The divisive 2016 presidential election and a local fight over public school funding that descended into name-calling had Zeiger thinking about how to teach citizens to civically talk to each other. Washington high schoolers are required by the state to take a half-credit in civics in order to graduate, but Zeiger worries that the civics they're getting is not of high quality, and it's not enough.

In the last two years, both Pacheco and Zeiger have championed bills to improve and expand civics education requirements in their states. Zeiger told the Everett, Washington, *Herald* that the breakdown in civic discourse rested at least somewhat on the backs of the schools. "The future of this country depends on our ability to resolve our differences in a civil and constructive way and that absolutely begins with civic education."[28]

Complacent and uninformed constituents and toxic political discourse have more states rethinking civics education programming; school leaders and legislators around the country have similar concerns and are taking a fresh look at civics requirements inside classrooms.

In the last couple of years, a little more than half of the states have at least considered bills or proposals to expand civics in schools in their most recent legislative sessions.[29] Many of the bills look to expand civics to younger students in elementary and middle schools, and some even include innovative new civics practices such as media literacy and action civics. As of 2018, only seven states include civics as part of a state accountability assessment, which means that in most states civics may not receive funding or emphasis (as many educators and school leaders have noted—"if it doesn't get tested, it doesn't get taught"). Figure 2.1, with data compiled by *Education Week*, details state-by-state requirements for civics, government, and U.S. history courses.

Nineteen states have opted to have students take some version of the U.S. citizenship test as a graduation requirement, due to the advocacy of a civic-minded nonprofit, the Joe Foss Institute. But among educators and civics experts, using the U.S. citizenship test as a measure of civic knowledge is controversial—some experts say learning basic facts about the birth of the country, the Constitution, and some U.S. history is often better than what most students get, which is close to nothing, while others say relying on one multiple-choice test for civic knowledge is reinforcing the kind of boring, rote civics that students have tuned out for decades.

In 2013, the National Council for the Social Studies completely revamped its framework for teaching history, geography, government, and civics, with a renewed emphasis not just on college and career but also civic life. In the new C3 framework, which more than 20 states have signed on to use to revamp their history and civics requirements, preparing students for citizenship focuses on inquiry and evidence-based studies, with a new push for students to participate in "informed action" or action civics projects—one of the key elements of the new civics.[30] Some states, including California, have borrowed some of the C3 framework, while the District of Columbia, Maryland, and Illinois have adopted the entire framework to rework state history and government standards to be more civics-centered.

Still other states are incorporating the six research-based proven practices published in the Civic Mission of Schools' *Guardian of Democracy* report discussed in chapter 1. The proven practices cover both traditional civics such as classroom instruction on the law, government, and the Constitution, and discussion of current events, as well as elements of the new civics, such as legislative simulations, media literacy, and action civics.[31]

A few states have gone above and beyond to make big investments in civics, like Florida. Florida has one of the most robust civics education laws in the country, the 2011 Sandra Day O'Connor Civics Education Act, which includes a requirement passing a year-long civics education course in middle school and an end-of-course exam. As mentioned earlier, Parkland activists Emma González and David Hogg were part of the first group of students to take the course in 2013.

State	Requires civics or government course	Course Span (years)	Requires civics exam to graduate	Requires U.S. history course	Course Span (years)	Requires U.S. History exam to graduate	Notes
Alabama	Y	0.5	Y	Y	2	N	
Alaska	N	NA	N	N	NA	N	
Arizona	Y	0.5	Y	Y	1	N	
Arkansas	Y	0.5	Y	Y	1	N	
California	Y	0.5	N	Y	1	N	
Colorado	Y	1	N	N	NA	N	
Connecticut	Y	0.5	N	N	NA	N	
Delaware	N	NA	N	Y	0.5-1	N	U.S. history is part of state social studies exam taken in Grade 11
District of Columbia	Y	0.5	N	Y	1	N	
Florida	Y	0.5	Y	Y	1	Y	Beginning in 2018-19, students entering Florida colleges and universities must either complete a course or pass a test in civics.
Georgia	Y	0.5-1	N	Y	1	Y	
Hawaii	Y	0.5	N	Y	1	N	
Idaho	Y	1	Y	Y	1	N	
Illinois	Y	0.5	N	Y	1	Y	
Indiana	Y	0.5	N	Y	1	N	
Iowa	Y	0.5	N	Y	1	N	
Kansas	Y	0.5	N	Y	1	N	
Kentucky	N	NA	Y	N	NA	N	Students must earn a total of 3 credits in social studies, including U.S. History and government. High school graduation requirements are currently in flux.
Louisiana	Y	0.5	Y	Y	0.5-1	N	Students must pass either the Biology 1 or U.S. History exam

State	Requires civics or government course	Course Span (years)	Requires civics exam to graduate	Requires U.S. history course	Course Span (years)	Requires U.S. History exam to graduate	Notes
Maine	N	NA	N	N	NA	N	Students are required to study citizenship, government, and U.S. history to graduate but those topics may be integrated in other courses.
Maryland	Y	1	N	Y	1	N	
Massachusetts	Y	Not specified	N	Y	Not specified	N	Students are required to study U.S. history to graduate, but the length of time is not specified.
Michigan	Y	0.5	N	N	NA	N	The Michigan Merit Curriculum (MMC) includes a history 3-credit requirement, but no course requirements to graduate. The Michigan Merit exam (MME) is the high school assessment that corresponding to those requirements in the standards.
Minnesota	N	NA	N	Y	Not specified	N	Students must have 3.5 credits of social studies, which includes U.S. history. Standards call for the equivalents of one year of civics.
Mississippi	N	NA	N	Y	1	Y	Students must take the U.S. History exam at the conclusion of the course, but a passing score is not required to graduate. Students may use several alternative options to demonstrate mastery of the content in order to graduate.
Missouri	Y	0.5	Y	Y	1	Y	
Montana	N	NA	N	N	NA	N	
Nebraska	N	NA	N	N	NA	N	U.S. history is part of required state standards. Students must take 3 years of social studies to graduate.
Nevada	Y	1	N	Y	1	N	Students will only take a semester of civics starting in 2022. Civics exam will be a graduation requirement starting in 2019.
New Hampshire	Y	0.5	Y	Y	1	N	
New Jersey	N	NA	N	Y	2	N	
New Mexico	Y	0.5	Y	Y	1	Y	
New York	Y	0.5	N	Y	1	Y	Students must pass a Regents exam in either Global History or U.S. History to graduate

State	Requires civics or government course	Course Span (years)	Requires civics exam to graduate	Requires U.S. history course	Course Span (years)	Requires U.S. History exam to graduate	Notes
North Carolina	Y	1	Y	Y	2-Jan	Y	
North Dakota	Y	0.5-1	Y	Y	1	Y	
Ohio	Y	0.5	Y	Y	0.5	Y	
Oklahoma	Y	0.5	N	Y	1	Y	
Oregon	N	NA	N	N	NA	N	
Pennsylvania	N	NA	N	Y	NA	N	Civics exam will be required starting in 2020.
Rhode Island	N	NA	N	N	NA	N	
South Carolina	Y	0.5	Y	Y	1	Y	
South Dakota	Y	0.5	N	Y	1	N	
Tennessee	Y	0.5	Y	Y	1	Y	
Texas	Y	0.5	N	Y	1.5	Y	
Utah	Y	0.5	Y	Y	1	N	
Vermont	N	NA	N	Y	NA	N	
Virginia	Y	1	N	Y	0.5-1	Y	
Washington	N	NA	N	Y	1	N	A civics exam and a civics stand-alone course will be required starting with the 2020-21 school year.
West Virginia	Y	1	Y	Y	1	N	Students must take at least three social studies credits, which includes some instruction in state and local government.
Wisconsin	N	NA	Y	N	NA	N	Students must take at least three social studies credits, which includes some instruction in state and local government.
Wyoming	Y	1	Y	Y	NA	N	Three school years of social studies, including history and American government, are required.

Figure 2.1. **What's required where: A state-by-state breakdown.** *Published with permission from "Most States Require History, Not Civics," Education Week, October 23, 2018.*

In 2018, after nearly two decades of failed attempts, the Massachusetts statehouse also passed a comprehensive civics education bill. The new law mandates civics courses for both middle and high school students, provides a Civics Budget fund to help schools pay for resources and professional development, and creates a program for high school voter registration. But perhaps most importantly, the bill specifies that the civics that is taught must be active and project oriented, and encourages student participation.

Arielle Jennings, the Massachusetts executive director of the nonprofit Generation Citizen, advocated strongly for the bill, especially to ensure project-based and action civics were requirements. "The traditional civics, with its crammed content on the three branches of government, really doesn't ensure that every kid gets what we call high-quality civics, which is about participation as well as content," she said in an interview. "Often the rich schools get the innovative stuff and the low-income students get the most rote civics learning, and the lowest standards of civics. Our work isn't just to bring civics back, but to bring it back for everyone."

In the long run, Florida's and Massachusetts's payoff for strengthening civics may be greater turnout at the voting booth—a key indicator in civic engagement. In a 2010 paper, Johns Hopkins researcher Jennifer Bachner looked at students who took a full year of civics or American government in school to see if they were more likely to vote. Bachner found that civics made a difference—students who took civics were 3 to 6 percentage points more likely to vote than those high schoolers who didn't. For students who didn't discuss politics at home with their parents, a full-year civics course had an even greater effect; they were anywhere from 7 to 11 percentage points more likely to vote than students who took no civics. According to Bachner, results suggest that civics in school could make up for "lack of political socialization at home."[32]

CIVICS EDUCATION IS NEEDED: LOOKING AHEAD

Civics education is a way to raise young people to be engaged citizens who vote, volunteer in their communities, and share the rights and responsibilities of democratic rule. And though civic knowledge, skills, and dispositions can be passed down to young people from a variety of channels—coaches, community leaders, pastors, rabbis, and, of course, parents—schools are by far the most reliable way to reach every child. Educating for citizenship was the original reason for creating the public school system, and over the last few years, legislators and school leaders have come to realize that schools are critical to spreading civics.

We know so far that the new century has created a new kind of young citizen—one who is culturally and racially diverse, always digitally connected, raised with polarized politics, and cares about social issues and making a difference in the world. And now we know that states and school districts are aware of the problem of a lack of civics education, and a handful are making an attempt to strengthen civics requirements—and the ones who have, like Florida, have already produced young people who are more civically engaged. What kind of civics education should be taught in the twenty-first century?

The next chapters will take a detailed look at the practices that make up the new civics, and how educators, schools, and programs are reshaping traditional civics instruction to meet the needs of their students, beginning first with a look at how schools teach history.

FOR TEACHERS TO THINK ABOUT

- Civics education was once the reason for and the purpose of American public schools, but has disappeared over the last 50 years. Reforms based on STEM education and a standardized testing movement focused on reading and math have contributed to ignoring civics as an important part of American education.
- Though most states require at least some kind of government or civics class in order to graduate, few have the kind of robust civics education, spread over multiple years and using the proven practices, that experts recommend for a healthy and civically engaged democracy.
- There is an unequal distribution of civics education: wealthier, whiter students get more and better civics education than do lower-income students and students of color. Not providing civics education to a large part of the American population creates a civics knowledge gap that leads to a *civic empowerment gap*—young people may not know how to take part in politics and their community.
- In the last few years, a few states like Massachusetts, Illinois, and Florida have invested heavily in civics education, including adding civics courses in middle school and new civics requirements such as media literacy courses and project-based action civics. Nineteen states have made the multiple-choice U.S. citizenship test a graduation requirement, but critics say that while it's a good start, more is required to teach students how to be engaged citizens.

FOR PARENTS TO THINK ABOUT

- Parents are the first and best civics teachers. They model good civic behavior such as voting and volunteering, and can engage kids in discussion of current events and political beliefs.

- Civics education is a vital and necessary part of American education, and belongs in school. Civics teaches young people how government works, how they can be involved, and why involvement matters. Not teaching civics has contributed to low political and government knowledge, low voter rates, and community disengagement. Even though reading and math standards and standardized testing have crowded out time for social studies, history, and civics, every school needs civics education at the elementary, middle, and high school level.

The chapter title comes from Horace Mann, who said "The common school is an integral part of the social order. . . . Common schools are nurseries of a free republic." Democracy and the Renewal of Public Education, *edited by Richard John Neuhaus (Grand Rapids, MI: William B. Eerdmans, 1987), 45.*

Chapter Three

New Civics Innovator

Seth Andrew, Democracy Prep, and the Civic Success Sequence

Seth Andrew grew up a politics kid. Both parents worked in politics, and growing up in Manhattan, public life and family life were intertwined as far back as he can remember. Andrew always knew he wanted to be involved in the workings of democracy somehow, so he experimented—first working as a congressional page while still in high school, and then taking the plunge and running for office while he was still in college.

But during his campaign for Rhode Island state representative while earning his undergraduate degree at Brown University, he was shocked to find that many voters didn't have the knowledge or passion for politics that he did. In the months before the election, Andrew knocked on doors and got to know the constituents in his district, a blend of three distinct cultures: affluent Brown families living near the university, college students, and Mt. Hope, a primarily working-class community of color. Though the groups were distinct, they had one thing in common: very few of them knew anything about state politics. Andrew quickly realized that he might be a politics unicorn.

Though he ended up losing the race by 79 votes, Andrew walked away from what he called the "brutal" campaign experience with two revelations: one, he didn't really want to be a politician, and two, most people don't know anything about their own government, and he had assumed that they did. He had assumed that people knew the difference between a state representative and a state council member, but he had been wrong. If his experience knocking on doors was any indication of the population at large, then he had taken his love for politics and government for granted. Politics as a career didn't pan out, but the experience ended up redirecting Andrew's aspirations toward getting at the root of the problem, which, Andrew grew to believe, was in schools. Schools were the most likely place to teach Americans civics, but in most schools it was either a failed attempt or absent altogether. And he decided to do something about it.

After a few years teaching and a fellowship that helped develop a charter school, in the fall of 2006 Andrew launched a new kind of charter middle school located in Harlem, New York City, that would make civics education not just a feature but the core mission of the school. Democracy Prep was one of the first schools of its kind. Andrew had drawn inspiration from other civics-focused schools like Roxbury Prep in Boston, founded by former Secretary of Education John King, and Douglas Academy in Harlem, but his idea to focus on civics education and citizenship instead of just test scores was an outlier. The school motto, "Work hard. Go to college. Change the world!" meshes the ideas of scholarship, academic success, and citizenship.

Andrew started as principal with a group of mostly African American and Latino low-income sixth graders from the surrounding neighborhoods. From the beginning, Andrew and his team, which included long-time former CEO Katie Duffy, wanted to make sure students understood that civics was the core of why they were there. They created the Friday town hall meeting, where the whole school would gather and hear talks about civic participation. They would often begin by reciting the Pledge of Allegiance, followed by the Democracy Prep pledge:

> I pledge allegiance to my future at Democracy Prep charter school
> And to the values for which it stands
> One team, under DREAM, with citizenship and scholarship for all.

(DREAM is an acronym representing the core values stated in the mission of the school: discipline, respect, enthusiasm, accountability, and maturity.)

As the school grew and expanded into high school, school leaders developed about 20 specific ways to inject civics education directly into all aspects the curriculum. Civics was woven into math and English language arts— Andrew recalled how civic knowledge can be reinforced in math class through problems like finding the percentages of Electoral College votes, or making fractions using the 435 members of the House of Representatives. They also developed a student-centered, get-out-the-vote campaign that was debuted on the sidewalks of Harlem. Before Election Day, groups of students wearing t-shirts stating "I can't vote, but you can!" help to register neighborhood voters and encourage adults to vote.

In their senior year, students take a required year-long capstone "Change the World" class, in which they design their own real-world civics project and then execute it. Since civic engagement happens as much online as it does in the streets, students are required to build an online platform to go along with their project and attract at least 100 followers to their cause. Many projects have an activist slant, and projects often consist of organizing protests and sit-ins, but in addition students must provide a detailed policy brief explaining what policy changes would help their cause, and how to go about making those changes—a crucial step that would not be possible without their extensive civic background knowledge in the detailed workings of the local, state, and national government.

The whole idea of Democracy Prep and the education it provides is innovative, yet Andrew bristles at the idea that there is a "twenty-first century" civics innovation that does not need knowledge of history and government, only "skills" such as practicing civic engagement, and good citizen behavior like cooperation and communication. In many ways, the innovation in Democracy Prep's style of teaching civics is that it's pretty traditional: the teachers want kids to know stuff before they attempt to do stuff. Even the best civic behaviors aren't worth much, according to Andrew, without a base level of civics knowledge. Andrew's quest for spreading civic knowledge makes him something of an outlier in civics education, and education in general—for many progressive educators, focusing too much on knowledge in the age of Google and unlimited streams of information seems outdated, old-fashioned, and even unnecessary. (David Ross at nonprofit P21, for example, who has in many ways led the charge to make civics education less knowledge focused and more skills focused, told me that historical knowledge can be used by kids for being good at Jeopardy, and not much else.)

But the more years Andrew has worked with kids, the more he has become convinced that if schools want to educate future citizens, there needs to be a floor of civics knowledge before other aspects of civics education—like the skills and dispositions that make kids more likely to grow up and participate—can be integrated. Through a couple of his sidebar nonprofits, Andrew had been behind a campaign to pass legislation to require that students pass the U.S. citizenship test in order to graduate, an initiative that has since been taken up by the Joe Foss Institute and has passed in 19 states. Though social studies and government educators have voiced concerns about the initiative, saying it rewards a kind of surface civics knowledge, Andrew said surface knowledge is better than *no* knowledge (remember from the introduction how few adults even know what the three branches of government are or can name any rights provided by the Constitution).

Many schools trying to incorporate civics education, he believes, are missing this crucial step. Without understanding history and the details of how government works, and without knowing the core principles of what America stands for, teaching civics skills will fail to produce engaged citizens.

At the first Democracy Prep commencement in 2013, he told the seniors, "We don't run the school like a democracy, we prepare you for one," referring to the progressive idea that if students are just exposed to democracy, they will somehow internalize it.

He's worried most about action civics, the student-directed projects that focus on taking civic action to address community problems (covered in more detail in chapter 13). Proponents of action civics say that allowing students to be part of the democratic process gives students a voice and instills in them an understanding and desire to participate that they can carry to adulthood. "Most schools using action civics have it exactly backwards," Andrew said. "They teach civic activism hoping kids will get hooked. I believe schools should teach the knowledge first, and then show them how to apply it in real ways over the course of a lifetime."

Democracy Prep teaches students to address big, systemic problems and gives them the detailed knowledge and the tools to solve them. For example, in 2008, two Democracy Prep students, a seventh grader and an eighth grader, testified before the New York State Senate on opposite sides of the issue of mayoral control of the city's schools. At the time, the city was engaged in a fiery debate over who got to control the schools, and whether the school board should be appointed by the mayor or elected by the people.

Each student was given three minutes, and even though their opinions differed in every way—one favored mayoral control, while the other believed in public control—their arguments were detailed and displayed confident knowledge about how the system worked. To Andrew and those at Democracy Prep, this kind of real debate will build better citizens. "They did it themselves, and they were involved in a real debate about a real issue, rather than debates around cafeteria menus and prom colors," Andrew said.

Out of these experiences, Andrew and the Democracy Prep team decided to come up with a way to build civic engagement in a series of steps, called the "civic success sequence," which is made up of three sequential elements: First, teach students civic knowledge about history and government, the Constitution, and the Bill of Rights. Once that knowledge is internalized, it leads to the explicit teaching of civic engagement skills, as demonstrated by the students testifying in front of the New York Senate (which Andrew said would have been a waste of time for both the students and those listening if the kids didn't know what they were talking about). Those civic skills over time become highly desired, lifelong civic dispositions, as evidenced by young people who decide to volunteer for a political campaign, participate in a public debate, become a part of their community politics, and register to vote.

Addressing the civics gap that impacts low-income and minority kids is a big part of Democracy Prep's mission. The school is committed to giving low-income students and students of color the kind of civics knowledge and skills that they often miss, effectively shutting them out of civic involvement in adulthood. But Andrew also wants to reach all the kids who aren't automatically attracted to civics and politics the way he was. Kids like him are already involved, participating in Model United Nations and taking the AP Government course. "We don't need to worry about those kids," Andrew said, "They will be fine."

The real test of whether or not Democracy Prep's style of civics education and the civics success sequence will affect students for the rest of their lives lies in the future. But a small study of graduates shows promising results.

In order to test Democracy Prep's effectiveness in producing more engaged citizens, in 2018 the policy research firm Mathematica conducted a preliminary study of the first cohort of Democracy Prep graduates to see whether they registered to vote and voted in higher numbers than the students who applied to the school but didn't attend. Though the sample size was small, analyst Brian Gill, one of the researchers on the study, said they found a "very large impact" on voter registration and voting.

Gill said that the researchers first looked at the demographics of Democracy Prep students: 76 percent of students qualified for free and reduced-price meals; the student body is 69 percent black and 30 percent Hispanic. Nearly a quarter of the students speak no English at home, and 17 percent were enrolled in special education. All these factors, Gill said, have been associated with low voter rates and low civic engagement in previous research. But students who enrolled in Democracy Prep had much higher voting rates than those who didn't: in a sample of students attending Democracy Prep for an average of four years, voter registration rates increased by 16 percent, and actual voting rates by 12 percent. The researchers concluded that there is a 98 percent probability that attending Democracy Prep increases voter registration rates and voting.[1]

"The impact is very large," Gill said. "The study provided for us what we call 'existence proof': that it is in fact possible to do something within schools to dramatically increase civic participation." Gill said to grasp the size of the impact, add the Democracy Prep numbers of 16 percent and 12 percent to the average voting rate of 18 to 24 year olds in the 2016 election, which hovered just under 50 percent—it would bump up youth voting rates significantly.

The next step, Gill said, would be to figure out exactly which parts worked to increase civic engagement so much. Educator and author Robert Pondiscio, who taught the Socratic-style "senior seminar" in civics and citizenship at Democracy Prep for two years, said that he believes the reason the school "works" is because the ethos of civics education is baked into every aspect of the school. Now that the school serves students from kindergarten through twelfth grade, the daily expectation that they be involved citizens becomes internalized by students.

Yet Andrew tends to think it's the accumulation of specific details—the inner workings of the civic success sequence—that produce the results. In the meantime, Gill said, until they understand exactly which aspects of the civics curriculum are producing results, schools could learn from what they are doing in order to increase voting rates within their populations.

Though encouraged by the study, Andrew was disappointed the numbers weren't even higher, and believes as the number of graduates grow, the numbers participating in civic life will also grow. "We now know this works, we know this is powerful, and I'm confident that it will be even more powerful on an even larger scale," he said.

Democracy Prep is now a large network of charters, 22 elementary, middle, and high schools located in New York, New Jersey, the District of Columbia, Baton Rouge, and Las Vegas. These schools serve more than 7,500 students. Andrew doesn't expect that every Democracy Prep student will grow up to be a politician or work in government, though that would be a nice side effect of the thorough civics education.

Although Andrew no longer plays a daily role in operations at Democracy Prep, he has gone on to build the same civic-minded schools in Liberia and other countries. He hopes that Democracy Prep can serve as an example for more schools to revive the original core mission of public schooling, and place civics education and raising citizens back at the hearts of their missions.

When I inquire about other subjects of interest, like the arts or STEM, Andrew assures me that there is still plenty of time for the arts and STEM and all the other programs that appeal to all kinds of parents and students at Democracy Prep without sacrificing the time for the incredibly focused civics curriculum. But those don't detract from making sure that every student understands their rights and responsibilities as Americans.

"For years, we've had an opt-in civics," he said, referring to the tech industry term for users who must go out of their way to sign up for a desired service or product. Andrew is looking for schools to be "opt-out" civics—a requirement that every student gets basic civic knowledge and skills, whether or not they are headed for a future in politics.

Chapter Four

A Tree without Roots

Repairing the History Knowledge Gap

Those who don't remember the past are condemned to repeat the eleventh grade.

—James W. Loewen

"There is little reason to believe that there ever was a golden age when students were well-versed in American history," wrote public school historian Diane Ravitch in an op-ed piece in the *New York Times*.[1] For all the talk about history's importance, and aphorisms suggesting we're "doomed to repeat" it, Ravitch wrote that a history test given to 7,000 college freshmen as far back as 1943 showed that fewer than one in four could name two achievements of Abraham Lincoln; only 6 percent could name the original 13 colonies.

Ravitch argued that history standards needed to be stronger, and explained a preliminary field test of a history assessment she helped develop for the NAEP (the "Nation's Report Card" discussed in chapter 2). The purpose of the new test was to assess how much eleventh graders knew about history, and a small sampling of students from various regions that took the test gave Ravitch a clue what students knew: not much. Two-thirds of the sample set couldn't correctly identify the time period during which the Civil War took place; one-third couldn't find Britain or France on a map of Europe; half didn't know what was meant by the *Brown* decision.

Schools ignore history at their peril, Ravitch wrote: "If knowledge of the past is in fact relevant to our ability to understand the present and to exercise freedom of mind—as totalitarian societies, both real and fictional, acknowledge by stringently controlling what may be studied or published, then there is cause for concern about many Americans' sense of history. The threat to our knowledge of the past comes, however, not from government censorship but from indifference and ignorance. The erosion of historical understanding seems especially pronounced among the generation under 35, those schooled during the period of sharp declines in basic skills."[2]

This blistering account of a nation without history was written not in the twenty-first century, but back in 1985—a time before the internet, fake news, and years before the narrowing of curriculum due to high-stakes testing. American schools are still struggling with delivering the most basic history knowledge today, and things may even have deteriorated since the 1980s. The last NAEP U.S. history test given to eighth graders in 2014 showed that only 17 percent of students scored "proficient" on the exam, while 53 percent scored at the "basic" level. Nearly one-third of students scored "below basic."[3] Though Americans have been worried about history knowledge for some time, the recent dismal test scores may reveal one great truth: American schools teach less history than they used to, especially in elementary schools.

Most elementary schools are hyper-focused on reading and math in order for students to perform well on state tests, leaving little more than 5 percent of instructional time spent on history or social studies[4]—the least time of all core subjects. This happens even more often in low-income schools, where reading and math scores tend to be lower.[5] When history and social studies courses do become more common, in middle and high school, students have little historic background knowledge to draw from, and the history they learn doesn't stick. Recent polls bear that out: most adults under the age of 45 don't know what year the Constitution was ratified or how many amendments it contains.[6] Even if knowing that date doesn't seem particularly important, current high schoolers don't know basic facts of U.S. history—such as slavery was the cause of the Civil War.[7] Two-thirds of young adults don't know what Auschwitz was, and 22 percent say they've never heard of the Holocaust.[8]

Critics of the current patched-together history curriculum—which varies from state to state, but most often consists of vague and meatless "social studies" in the early grades that often spills over into middle school—say that poor knowledge of history disengages students from learning about the victories and mistakes of the past, over time making these young people apathetic to the political process. When serious history courses do appear later in a student's school career, it's often too late to put knowledge into a context for historical understanding. Students also report that they find history "boring"—by adolescence, history often becomes an add-on, a long and arduous list of names and dates that teens say isn't relevant to their lives. A Gallup youth survey from 2003 showed that only 10 percent of American teens cite history as their favorite subject.[9]

A deep understanding of history was one of the founding goals of public education. The founders hoped that learning the lessons of history would prevent against future tyranny as well as allow citizens to exercise the "freedom of mind" Ravitch wrote about. Learning about the fall of Rome or the rise of the Third Reich provides citizens an incentive to be civically engaged—a reminder that the freedoms of our democratic republic are choices continually made at the ballot box.

Though Americans may have never known a lot of history, today many schools are teaching less and less, especially elementary schools. In order to improve civic engagement, young people need a stronger background in social studies and history—both for understanding the circumstances of the present and for exercising their freedom of mind.

WHEN HISTORY EDUCATION IS ELEMENTARY

On a rainy Wednesday in Nashville, Tennessee, Kayla Nicholson starts off her second-graders' day with a song. With students assembled on a rug at the front of the room and a plastic crown of laurel leaves around her head, Nicholson sings first a song about the ancient Greeks. It's a kind of call-and-response, half rap and half singsong that sounds more than a little like Meghan Trainor's "All About That Bass," which Nicholson has cleverly changed to "All About the Greeks."

"*A de-moc-ra-cy,*" everyone chants together, "*is a gov-ern-ment where the peo-ple-chooooooose their leader.*" They go on to do the same call-and-response singing with the definition of government as well as the ancient Greek city-states, Athens and Sparta, and their characteristics. The songs have lively, choreographed hand movements, like cheerleaders with jazz hands, that Nicholson and the students do together; the students know all the words.

The second graders are learning about the birth of democratic government, taught through a memorable song at a level they can understand. Students do this every morning as part of their "Listening and Learning" story time at Nashville Classical Charter School on Nashville's east side. The Listening and Learning content blocks rotate between science and history topics, with the goal of giving the students something specific: concrete knowledge about the world.

Nashville Classical, which serves largely low-income and minority students and currently goes from kindergarten to fifth grade (and will eventually go to eighth grade, as the school adds a class each year) uses the Core Knowledge curriculum, created by educator and knowledge proponent E. D. Hirsch Jr. Core Knowledge runs from kindergarten through eighth grade and aims to feed elementary students cold, hard facts: Who were the Athenians, and what did they accomplish? When was the concept of democracy founded, and by whom? This is something many schools now shy away from, not wanting to "drill and kill" their students with monotonous memorization. Yet the students in Ms. Nicholson's class don't look drilled—they are having fun, belting out things like *"The Spartans were waaaaaarriors"* in unison, biceps curved upward into muscles, with so much enthusiasm it rattles the floorboards.

Nicholson follows up the song with a story about Athens as the birthplace of democracy, which she reads from a book and shows pictures. Noticeably missing from the story is the standard elementary school text analysis: Nicholson doesn't ask the students to "find the main idea" of the story or "draw inferences" commonly seen in other classrooms, though Nicholson does stop periodically to call on students, asking them to explain what they just heard; the goal, however, seems to be for the children to learn the stories by heart. (They will later return to their seats and do some writing, answering reflective questions about what they just learned in the story.) The singsong raps and stories aren't just fun, but research-backed ways to help students remember what they learned, said Nashville Classical founder and Head of School Charlie Friedman.

Why should eight year olds learn the details of ancient Greek history? As Friedman winds me through the close hallways of Nashville Classical's (appropriately) 100-year-old building, talking excitedly about the importance of teaching students background knowledge, he said that sufficient knowledge of history provides students with two things: a foundation used to build more sophisticated thinking in history classes later on, and more broadly, a key to the middle class.

Friedman said his own Manhattan private-school education emphasized knowledge early (he later graduated from Yale with honors). And before the school opened, he did a lot of research, landing on E. D. Hirsch's philosophy: acquiring knowledge is central to further learning. He read books about learning by cognitive scientists, which showed him that the skills all educators want for their students, "critical thinking" and "problem solving" and the like, couldn't happen if students *didn't have anything to think about*.[10]

By the time we arrive at the door of a fifth-grade classroom, where students are using a more sophisticated history assignment to work on their writing, Friedman was talking about how history knowledge and democracy are intertwined. Friedman is concerned that the school's historically underserved population—Nashville Classical serves primarily low-income students and students of color—are often deprived of the experiences, like trips to museums and family vacations, that build broader knowledge about the world and are needed to be part of the middle class. Building that knowledge helps to create a common language for all citizens to use, "mental furniture"[11] that can then help students think about what to do about challenges in the future. If a large portion of Americans don't know what caused the Civil War, for example, then how can they come together to find common solutions to the issues of systemic racism today? How can Americans begin to discuss—or vote on—other challenges that face society when some citizens don't have the background knowledge to understand the context of those important conversations and decisions?[12]

Friedman said the knowledge and middle-class connection is vital to civic engagement—being a high school and college graduate makes citizens more likely to vote and volunteer,[13] and civic knowledge is correlated with more civic participation and "expression of democratic values."[14] Without the background of history, students often get left out of the most important conversations about how to live in a democracy.

"Background knowledge matters to civics education because our children can't build our future without reading and knowing our history," Friedman said. Core Knowledge curriculum is sequenced in a cycle and built like a layer cake, so events of history get returned to again and again, each time layering more context and age-appropriate understanding. When the topic of ancient Greece the second graders are studying comes up again in sixth grade, students will already know how to find it on a map and remember the framework of what the country was about, even if small details are forgotten. As a result, Friedman said, "Our students have a common language to discuss the world."

Though the Core Knowledge curriculum is backed by substantial research on how students learn and is used sporadically in some schools, it isn't that common. Most American elementary schools no longer spend significant time learning the basic facts of history.

Why Students Don't Know Much History

A few years ago, education journalist Natalie Wexler became curious as to why the harrowing achievement gap—the learning gap that exists between racial groups as well as between low-income students and their wealthier peers[15]—wasn't narrowing, despite so much concerted effort to address the problem. Focused mostly on differences between low-income and middle-class or wealthy students, through her research and reporting Wexler found that the term *achievement gap* concealed the real issue: that there is a stark *knowledge gap* between the two groups. She wrote about the disparity in a new book, *The Knowledge Gap*, and, according to Wexler, elementary schools have not been focused on building students' knowledge—especially in areas like history—for decades, instead focusing on teaching students mostly *skills*.[16]

For example, when teaching reading in the early grades, teachers need to focus on the skill of decoding, or learning to sound out different combinations of letters to form words. But once students learn to decode words, reading comprehension is also treated as a skill, and much of reading time throughout the rest of elementary school is taken up with efforts to build comprehension skills. Comprehension practice involves students reading books or texts about a variety of unconnected topics—ponies one day, how ice gets made another—and asks them to *do* things with the passages like "find the main idea" or "make inferences about the text." But Wexler discovered a well-established body of scientific evidence showing that the most important factor in reading comprehension isn't "skill," but how much background knowledge and vocabulary the reader has about the topic. If readers can't understand a passage, they can't apply a skill like "finding the main idea." Standardized tests present kids with passages on a range of topics that aren't tied to anything they might have learned in school, so often students with more general background knowledge are more likely to understand the passages, and do better on the tests.

Wexler pointed to a 1988 study on reading about the subject of baseball by researchers Donna Recht and Lauren Leslie.[17] The researchers took a group of junior high students and divided them into four groups:

- a group with high reading ability who also had a lot of prior knowledge about baseball
- a group with high reading ability who knew nothing about baseball
- a group with low reading ability who knew a lot about baseball
- a group with low reading ability who knew nothing about baseball

Recht and Leslie asked the students to read a passage about a half-inning of a baseball game, and then describe what they read and reenact the passage using figures on a baseball diamond. The researchers found that prior knowledge about the game of baseball, not reading ability, heavily influenced how well the students performed: students who were considered poor readers but knew a lot about baseball performed better than those who were good readers but knew nothing about baseball.

Wexler found that classrooms serving students from all income levels and backgrounds were prioritizing skills over building knowledge, but students from low-income backgrounds suffered the most from this approach. While children from wealthier families, whose parents generally tended to be more educated, picked up the kind of background knowledge that would help them succeed in school through their home environments, for a variety of reasons children from low-income families didn't have the same experiences. Low-income students relied on schools to provide that knowledge, and when their schools failed to provide it, they fell farther behind every year.

The focus on skills over building knowledge has only grown since strict reading and math accountability measures were introduced in the early

2000s, because the reading portion of the standardized tests consists of reading short passages and then finding the main idea and making inferences, leading schools to believe that the trick to doing well is learning how to find the main idea. The focus on raising test scores means that schools with the lowest performing kids are often doubling down on teaching comprehension skills. But "the kids who need knowledge the most through school are the ones who are least likely to get it," Wexler said in a phone interview. "Their schools are the most likely to have low scores on tests, therefore their schools are focusing on these illusory skills because they think it's going to raise test scores. It's not."

Knowledge is also needed for critical thinking, one of the essential seven survival skills introduced in chapter 1. According to cognitive scientist Daniel Willingham, "Factual knowledge enhances cognitive processes like problem solving and reasoning. The richer the knowledge base, the more smoothly and effectively these cognitive processes—the very ones that teachers target—operate. So, the more knowledge students accumulate, the smarter they become."[18] Thinking about any topic is bound up with background knowledge about that topic, and Willingham wrote that if a teacher asks a student to look at an issue from multiple perspectives, "if he doesn't know much about an issue, he *can't* think about it from multiple perspectives."[19]

But background knowledge isn't the only thing missing from elementary schools' history programs, noted Wexler—students are also robbed of time. Most school days are focused on reading and math, with little time for social studies, though teachers often try to fit it in, sometimes through their English Language Arts curriculum. But social studies lessons often eschew actual history, opting instead for more of a vague blend of lessons about self, community, geography, and inspiring stories about historical figures—all positive things, taken separately.

But Wexler said what ends up happening with so little time is that history learning gets boiled down to a "taste." Consider a third-grade class reading a biography of Harriet Tubman: "It's great to read about Harriet Tubman and her life, but if your students don't know anything about the Civil War, who was fighting and what they were fighting for, or about the Underground Railroad, then the knowledge won't stick," Wexler said in an interview. "Knowledge is like Velcro; it needs to stick to other related knowledge." Knowledge has a cumulative effect, snowballing over time.

So when Kayla Nicholson was singing "All About Those Greeks" with her second graders, rapping about where the idea of democracy came from, she was providing them with the "mental furniture" to make future thinking about history easier. She was also giving them the raw materials for harder work in history later on, when older students begin learning about the more complex problems of democracy.

A LIVING DEMOCRACY: HISTORY COMING ALIVE FOR THE TWENTY-FIRST CENTURY

In a comprehensive 2017 study of what students know about American slavery, the Southern Poverty Law Center found that high schoolers don't know much. Less than 10 percent of surveyed seniors were able to identify slavery as the central cause of the Civil War, and the majority didn't know that a constitutional amendment ended it. In addition, researchers found that classrooms and textbooks didn't cover slavery adequately, and teachers were often uneasy with "open-ended questions" about slavery. The Law Center concluded that slavery is often taught without context, and history courses emphasize so-called "positive" stories of the lives of Frederick Douglas or brave abolitionists without "understanding how slave labor built the nation."[20] The history curriculum they found also often accentuated the "progressive view of American history that can acknowledge flaws only to the extent that they have been addressed and solved."[21]

Slavery isn't the only topic that routinely receives uneven treatment in history class: the life of Helen Keller, the significance of Native Americans, and the Vietnam War are just a few topics that historians have indicated get the selective, glazed-over treatment in school history books, often presented without the whole story or proper context.[22] Though there's not nearly enough time in history class to cover every topic deeply, American history has always been a fight between facts and myth, the desire to weave a story of exceptional greatness and the inability to agree on exactly what the American story is, and how to teach it. (If there's any doubt about this, just Google "Texas history standards" and read about the years-long statewide slugfest over what does and does not get included in state history books,[23] or a similar partisan battle in Michigan over whether schools should refer to America as a "democracy" or a "constitutional republic."[24])

But the broader narrative that the United States of America tells through the events of its history—and nowhere more so than inside history classrooms—is directly connected to a civic purpose: who are we as Americans? What do we stand for? What are our values? How do we live together if we can't even agree on the facts? In an article in *Education Week*, journalist Stephen Sawchuk asked, "What if the inability of Americans to agree on our shared history—and on the right way to teach it—is a cause of our current polarization and political dysfunction, rather than a symptom?"[25]

But what if putting controversies at the center of teaching of American history is, for students, a feature and not a bug? Historian James Loewen, author of *Lies My Teacher Told Me: Everything Your American History Textbook Got Wrong*, wrote that "history is furious debate informed by evidence and reason."[26] A new generation of high school history programs wants to make those furious debates the centerpiece of the curriculum, asking students to study history and be the ones to make crucial decisions of democracy.

The Case Study Method

It's 1877, and two African American teenagers in Virginia are on trial for murder. Reconstruction has just ended, and the boys are found guilty in multiple trials by all-white juries. Then a federal judge intervenes and questions whether or not the verdicts can be legitimate—would the results have been different if the juries weren't composed of only white jurors? The case ended up in the Supreme Court, and is now front and center in Eleanor Cannon's eleventh-grade U.S. history class at St. John's School in Houston, Texas. Cannon's students are looking at the case and trying to decide how they would rule if they had been sitting on the Supreme Court over a century ago.

Cannon has been teaching the case—which examines the public roles of African Americans after Reconstruction as well as the role juries play in American democracy—for four years, and each year, she watches as students move from saying they hate history to becoming deeply and often emotionally engaged in debating cases like this one. After a couple of days researching the background of the era and original documents, they move on to the case itself, Cannon told me that she gets to ask them the "big questions" about history, such as "what is justice?" Students then debate what should be done in the case, backing up their statements and claims with evidence. The arguments become intense, even emotional. Eventually, Cannon said, the class decides that the conviction of the black teens by an all-white jury is a violation of the Fourteenth Amendment, but then the hard work begins: so what's an appropriate amount of black jurors? One? Two? How do the courts decide, exactly, what makes a fair jury?

This legal case asks critical questions about American democracy, offering high schoolers a chance to participate in the hard decisions of governing, and is part of a program created by Harvard professor David Moss. Moss wants high schoolers to know that democracy isn't a set of cut-and-dried rules, but a series of decisions made by real people and a constant refining of values.

The class began as an undergraduate course called "History of American Democracy," and Moss designed it as the history version of the Harvard Business School "case study" method of teaching, in which students research a particular problem of an already established business, and then make a prediction about what outcomes would be recommended based on the facts at hand. Moss's idea was to do the same with history: take a particular, crucial moment in American history and have students decide: What would I have done in that situation? What was the preferred outcome, and why?

"History of American Democracy" quickly became one of the most popular classes at Harvard, and students professed that the way Moss presented the information, in the form of an argument for or against a certain ruling, made them retain it better. Cannon also said that arguments made the information "sticky" and students tended to remember it. Some of Moss's undergraduates reported becoming more civically engaged, with one even reportedly saying, "If this class didn't make every student in it a better citizen, I don't know what class would."[27] Moss said that one reason case studies are so interesting is that a case study puts "history in the present tense,"[28] providing students with a real-life democratic dilemma at a turning point in U.S. history, and asking them to make the decision.

Since 2015, Moss has re-created the cases for high schoolers like the ones in Cannon's class. Now called the Case Method Project, Moss is serving more than 200 teachers in 25 states hungry to make history come alive for their students, and hoping to expand the project. Initial student surveys show that students prefer learning history this way, and have even indicated that learning through the case method has made them more interested in civic life, like voting and even running for public office someday.

Maybe the case method is such a successful method of teaching history because it's exciting, but for many students history and government remain stuck in basic elements. As Moss notes, "The three branches of government are extremely important, the checks and balances are extremely important, the Bill of Rights is extremely important. But if you stop there, you miss almost the whole thing. Those are crucial pieces, to be sure, but by themselves they're not enough. Much more is needed for a successful democracy. We know this because if you try to export just those pieces, including the blueprint, the Constitution, to another country you don't get a working democracy."[29]

Cannon has been teaching history for more than two decades and has never experienced the depth of learning or critical thinking that happens when she's teaching the case method. She thinks deep learning happens in part because students see the historical players as people. "These are really the stories of people and the choices they make, and sometimes it's just the lesser of two evils," Cannon said. "But in each of the cases, whether it's James Madison or Martin Luther King Jr., you can really see agency. These historical and political figures from the history books are actually people, and the choices they make can make a difference. I think that can really increase students' civic engagement—there are good things about our system and there are challenges, but if you want to address a challenge you'll need to *do something* in order to do that. Sometimes the solutions work, and sometimes they don't, but let's learn about why it didn't work."

Over the last decade, movements like the Stanford History Education Group's "Reading Like a Historian," in which students investigate historical questions by reading and analyzing primary source documents, and the "Re-booting of Social Studies," history teacher Greg Milo's plan to create a more experiential history course for high schoolers, give students the opportunity to evaluate historical issues from different perspectives.

This kind of historical inquiry doesn't just make history more exciting or relevant to students—which is helpful—but also serves a civic purpose. The DBQ (Document-Based Questions) Project uses primary sources as a way to teach students to think like a historian through intensive, argument-based writing instruction. Students study primary documents from a historic event and then must make a claim that they support with evidence and reasoning. Using evidence to support your beliefs and ideas is a critical twenty-first-century civic skill, said one of DBQ's creators, Chip Brady, in an interview—one that's relevant to all kinds of big challenges society faces, from climate change to gun control. "You want kids to build this structure into their thinking about all the issues in their life: claim, evidence, reasoning. What we're doing is making that thinking visible through their writing."

The study of history and civics are closely linked. Not only does a detailed history of the United States give students an understanding of how the country was founded and what the ideas were behind its inception, but knowledge of the history of the world is necessary to understand current challenges and current events. The American Historical Association has written that economics, sociology, immigration, foreign trade, international relations, world resources, and "dozens of other" topics and areas of study cannot be understood without a knowledge of history.[30] A better understanding of history may also play a part in helping young citizens appreciate American values, since many simply don't know what they are, and understand the root causes of modern problems. Without history, civics is incomplete.

FOR TEACHERS TO THINK ABOUT

- Instruction in history and government is the foundation of student learning in civics education and the first of the proven practices outlined in the *Guardian of Democracy* report. Classroom time in civics, history, and government provides opportunities for aspects of the new civics, such as discussions of current events, media literacy, and action civics. Learning history and the workings of government can incorporate several of the seven survival skills for the twenty-first century such as critical thinking and problem solving, effective oral and written communication, and analyzing information.

- Most elementary schools don't have much time for social studies because it has been squeezed out for reading and math. And when classrooms do have social studies, real history is often shortchanged. In order to raise knowledgeable citizens, elementary school students need both time and content devoted to both social studies and history.

- Background knowledge in history can make learning more history easier, more engaging, and has the side effect of improving reading scores. Sufficient background knowledge in history also provides a solid foundation for later civic engagement.
- Innovative ways of teaching history like the case method put students in the driver's seat and ask them to answer the hard questions of democracy.

FOR PARENTS TO THINK ABOUT

- Knowledge is like Velcro: the more you have, the better new knowledge can stick. If your child doesn't get much history knowledge at school, think about ways to incorporate it at home, through local trips to historic sites, books or audiobooks about history, or educational videos such as Curiosity Stream.
- History education is not given the attention it deserves, especially in elementary school, but it makes for better readers and better citizens. Consider advocating for more, better history at your school.

The chapter title comes from Marcus Garvey, who stated, "A people without the knowledge of their past history, origin, and culture is like a tree without roots."

Chapter Five

New Civics Innovator

iCivics: Engaging the Twenty-First-Century Kid with Video Games

When Louise Dubé's son was in the fourth grade in 2012, he came home one afternoon and told her that he needed to play a video game for his social studies homework. She told him to finish his homework first, and then he could play the video game. "But mom," he said, "the homework *is* the game."

After disappearing to do his "homework" on the computer, Dubé's son returned and announced that "all of school" should be just like that video game. The boy who usually had to be bribed to finish homework wanted to keep playing, even though the game's subject matter was how to win an election—not exactly Mario Kart.

The game Dubé's son was playing was *Win the White House*, one of the most popular games on the civics learning site iCivics. Players in *Win the White House* get to create their own candidate, raise campaign funds, campaign and debate, and make it through the primaries to the general election. Dubé, a former attorney who was working in educational technology, was intrigued by the power of the game to keep her son playing until he figured out how to win, all while teaching him important civics concepts about elections. She wondered what features made the game interesting enough for a 10 year old to spend his free time playing a video game about politics. When she met the directors of the game a few years later, Dubé was so excited about the game that she came on board as executive director of the program.

iCivics was created to engage twenty-first-century kids through video games. The games give players, who range in age from 10 through late teens,

53

agency in making decisions about democracy—whether it's how to write laws in *Branches of Power* or how they would decide Supreme Court cases in *Argument Wars*.

Players of the site's most popular game, *Do I Have a Right?* run their own law firm that specializes in constitutional law. Clients come in with questions about legal challenges, such as whether a police officer had the right to confiscate the phone of a bus rider without accusing the person of a crime. Players determine whether the client has a right, and take cases to trial based on their knowledge of the Bill of Rights. The more cases players win, the bigger the law firm gets, and players can add special features to their offices, like an aquarium or a cat.

iCivics was the brainchild of former Supreme Court justice Sandra Day O'Connor, who took up the case of revitalizing civics education after she retired in 2006. After hearing from educators on their desire to use digital technology to update civics, O'Connor and her former clerk, Julie O'Sullivan, began looking into ways to create an "interactive" civics curriculum for middle schoolers. But it was eventually O'Sullivan's brother who suggested the idea of a civics video game.[1]

Though Justice O'Connor didn't know much about the internet or video games herself—one of O'Sullivan's anecdotes recalled that when she showed the former justice what a hyperlink was, she exclaimed, "Oh Julie, that's so clever!"[2]—she knew her grandchildren loved to play them. O'Connor heard from researcher James Gee, author of *What Video Games Have to Teach Us about Learning and Literacy*, about how video games could take a curriculum of facts and turn them into tools to help young people solve challenges—just the kind of engagement tool needed for subjects that students viewed as "boring," like civics. O'Connor told tech entrepreneur Asi Burak, creator of Israeli-Palestinian game *PeaceMaker* and author of *Power Play*, that she didn't need to see research; she wanted to use video games because she wanted children to be engaged.[3]

There is no doubt that video games engage young people; a recent survey from the Pew Research Center's Internet and American Life Project concluded that nearly all American kids—97 percent of boys and 83 percent of girls—play video games for fun.[4] Researchers who study games argue that well-designed video games can make kids smarter, become better problem-solvers, and even figure out answers to intractable social problems like obesity, conflicts between countries, and, yes, how the three branches of government work.

With the power and popularity of video games behind them, iCivics used digital technology to make civics fun. Since its launch in 2009, iCivics now offers 20 civics games in English and Spanish, and more than 170 civics lesson plans, all for free. The game is used by more than 200,000 teachers and 6.3 million students across the country. In the month of November 2016 alone, during the presidential election, students downloaded more than 3 million games.

In 2018, at age 88, O'Connor announced she was stepping away from public life for health reasons. Supreme Court Justice Sonia Sotomayor has since joined the board of iCivics, and is active in engaging a new generation of students in civics education. Since joining the board, Sotomayor has been a driving force behind getting the games translated into Spanish as well as supporting struggling readers. She has promised to take O'Connor's vision and move forward toward achieving her dream of remaking civics education for the twenty-first-century kid.[5]

Chapter Six

The Value of Virtue

Raising Citizens with Character

In all their relationships present and future . . . the greatest need of our boys and girls is character. . . . Not simply to learn to tell the truth or to respect property rights, but to realize in ever more vital ways that the worth of life consists in the endeavor to live out in every sphere the conduct of the noblest of which one is capable—this it is which gives education its highest meaning.
—*Moral Values in Secondary Education*, 1918

Reading, writing and arithmetic are important only if they serve to make our children more humane.
—Haim Ginott

In a nationwide survey of more than 70,000 high school students conducted between 2002 and 2015, 64 percent of teens admitted to cheating on a test, and 58 percent said they had plagiarized in a paper.[1] Smartphones, apparently, make cheating easier: in a different survey, one-third of students admitted to storing answers on their phone to view during a test, or texting friends for an answer.[2] A quarter of those students reportedly didn't even realize that using a phone during a test constituted cheating. Common Sense Media founder James Steyer said the cheating numbers "should be a wake-up call for educators and parents. These versatile technologies have made cheating easier."[3]

Cheating at school isn't the only kind of bad behavior making headlines: social media has made uncivil bullying and hateful behavior widely available to all, easily viewed and shared. Celebrities with large followings and people in positions of power, often seen as role models, take to social media to engage in name-calling and harassment. Character failures have become

57

widely shared social media events, like when a writer for TV's "Saturday Night Live" tweeted to her more than 20,000 followers that Barron Trump, President Trump's son, "will be this country's first homeschool shooter";[4] a candidate for Congress in Montana assaulted a reporter for asking him a question (and later won the election).[5] President Donald Trump has joined in the kind of social media name-calling and public shaming that parents say they try to discourage in their own children: one of his most popular and widely shared tweets was a video of him punching and wrestling a "person" with a CNN logo for a face.

Though Twitter shaming and humiliating YouTube videos can set bad examples for young people that they may try to emulate, a darker side to bad behavior can have much more serious consequences. According to the Centers for Disease Control and Prevention, bullying both online and off remains a serious problem for adolescents. Though reported incidents of bullying have decreased slightly over the last decade, a stubborn 20 percent of adolescents report being bullied for their physical appearance, race, gender, disability, religion, or sexual orientation.[6]

Meanwhile, hate incidents within schools are on the rise. The 2017 Federal Bureau of Investigation Hate Crime Statistics Report showed a large jump in bias-motivated violence over the last two years—rising by nearly 25 percent each year, for two straight years in a row.[7] Though some of the increase may be attributed to better and more accurate reporting, as the FBI's civil rights division made hate crimes a top priority in 2016, anecdotal reports among education leaders indicate an increase in swastikas, Nazi salutes, and anti-black racism inside schools.[8] In a news report, Maureen Costello, director of Teaching Tolerance at the Southern Poverty Law Center, explained that the increase is no surprise to her, considering all the hateful incidents swirling through social media and the news, from teachers wearing anti-immigrant Halloween costumes in an Idaho school to the anti-Semitic-motivated murder of 11 people at the Tree of Life Synagogue in Pittsburgh. "The children in our schools are simply reflecting the divisions we're seeing throughout America," Costello said. "The danger is that children may learn that hate and extremism are normal, and that bullying and violence are acceptable."[9]

Though bad behavior and moral failings have always existed in public life, and parents and educators have wanted to raise children of good character since the beginning of time, the twenty-first century presents an entirely new set of character challenges. What feels different today is the prominence of unethical and immoral behavior—occurring mostly through the unending streams on our smartphones. Unethical, mean, and harassing behavior has become part of the background noise of our lives, and psychologists say it's leaping off the screen and seeping into real life as well. "We are normalizing [these] behaviors, and it's affecting some kids," said child psychologist

Catherine Steiner-Adair, author of *The Big Disconnect: Protecting Childhood and Family Relationships in the Digital Age.*[10]

Developmental psychologist Marvin Berkowitz, a codirector of the Center for Character and Citizenship at the University of Missouri–St. Louis, said that for too long parents and educators have ignored what he calls "the moral part of the equation."

"If we don't address it," he said in an interview, mincing no words, "we are going to take the whole world down." Society both in and out of schools has ignored moral virtues like goodness, honesty, compassion, and wisdom for far too long, Berkowitz said, believing that moral virtues are too tied to religion. And we are now paying the price, on social media and in the public sphere, in classrooms and on the playground. While parents and caregivers are usually the first and most important educators to help children develop character, Berkowitz notes that for the last few decades in schools, the pendulum of character education has swung too far in the direction of what he calls "performance virtues," character traits associated with accomplishing goals, like confidence, teamwork, perseverance, and "grit." While these character traits are important, they're just one part of the "Building Blocks of Character" described below that create a full and well-rounded character education. Intellectual virtues like curiosity and resourcefulness; civic virtues like service, volunteering, and promoting the common good; and the moral virtues have been crowded out—"crushed," Berkowitz said—by schools' singular pursuit of developing character traits that lead to academic success.

THE BUILDING BLOCKS OF CHARACTER[11]

- *Intellectual virtues*: Character traits necessary for discernment, right action, and the pursuit of knowledge, truth, and understanding. Examples include critical thinking and curiosity, judgment, reasoning, and resourcefulness.
- *Moral virtues*: Character traits that enable us to act well in situations that require an ethical response. Examples include compassion, gratitude, honesty, humility, justice, and respect.
- *Civic virtues*: Character traits that are necessary for engaged responsible citizenship, contributing to the common good. Examples include citizenship, civility, community awareness, service, and volunteering.
- *Performance virtues*: Character traits that have an instrumental value in enabling the intellectual, moral, and civic virtues. Examples include confidence, determination, motivation, perseverance, resilience, and teamwork.

Performance virtues are at the heart of "grit," the now-famous education term coined by psychologist Angela Duckworth, who studied high achievers to uncover the secrets of their success. She found that students' "non-cognitive skills" such as self-control and conscientiousness were a greater predictor of school success than IQ or other cognitive measures of smarts. Students who have grit, which Duckworth herself defines as "perseverance and passion for long-term goals," have higher grade point averages and graduate at higher rates. [12]

Eager to land on a strategy to increase performance, schools and districts quickly embraced the idea that non-cognitive skills like grit could help students achieve their academic goals. Spurred on by Paul Tough's book, *How Children Succeed*,[13] federal law was updated to require districts to include at least one measure of non-academic skills as part of their accountability measures, and districts quickly began adopting programs to teach and measure empathy, self-control, and social awareness, often called social-emotional learning, or SEL.

Performance virtues are certainly important, not just in school performance, but for success in life; yet Duckworth has urged caution on programs that teach skills like "grit," as well as non-cognitive tests tied to high-stakes measurements of student and school performance, saying "they weren't created for this purpose,"[14] and that more research is needed.

While a large, well-established body of research has shown that students benefit from well-implemented social-emotional learning programs, and that such programs improve skills like responsible decision-making and social awareness, decrease undesirable behavior, and improve students' attitudes about school,[15] performance-related virtues can't be considered the only virtues worth teaching. In the quest to achieve maximum performance, schools, parents, and society in general have become fixated on virtues of performance, and may have even warped young people's attitudes toward these virtues. Some have suggested that too much emphasis on performance virtues without distinguishing the good and bad ways perseverance can be used can backfire; one journalist quipped, "While it takes grit and self-control to be a successful heart surgeon, the same could be said about a suicide bomber."[16]

Students have told researchers that their performance matters more to their parents than being a good person, no matter what their parents may say. In a 2014 study of 10,000 American middle and high school students, when asked whether it was more important to achieve at a high level, achieve happiness, or care for others, nearly 80 percent of students said that achieving at a high level mattered more than caring for others. They also said their parents valued their achievement more than if they spent their time caring for others, creating a gap between what parents say they want for their children and the "real messages they convey in their behavior day to day."[17]

"We've come to think of schools as purely college prep and workforce development institutions, and we've forgotten they're also about helping kids flourish as whole human beings and future citizens," Marvin Berkowitz said. "Productive members of society aren't simply smart people with lots of factoids in their brains. Nothing is more important than the formation of moral people. There's no moral future without children of character. We will live in a far better world if we take this to heart."

Over the last few years, Berkowitz said, he's seen increased interest from both educators and the public to begin helping children imagine and build that "far better world" of the other three virtues, especially moral virtues, most likely because adults are watching ethical and moral behavior slip away. Social media takedowns, 24/7 news cycles, rampant lies and conspiracy theories, hostile and confrontational public shaming, bullying, and hateful behavior all have grownups rethinking the messages that young people are receiving constantly through their phones. As a result, there's been a nationwide resurgence in schools and districts thinking more intentionally about how to implement a positive, safe, and welcoming school culture and climate that research has shown to decrease bullying and bad behavior. In addition, many social-emotional learning programs also teach moral virtues, like empathy.

Berkowitz said that swinging the pendulum back from performance virtues toward moral virtues can be vital to improving civic and ethical behavior. Though he's concerned that schools are already overwhelmed with everything they are trying to do, he said that placing value in moral education shouldn't be considered "just another thing to put on a school's plate." Moral education, he said, *is* the plate.

TAKING CARE OF OTHERS AS CIVIC VIRTUE

Two weeks before Christmas, the teachers at Muskogee Early Childhood Center in Muskogee, Oklahoma, loaded 150 four year olds onto school buses and headed out of downtown to the Walmart Supercenter for a special kind of holiday party. The preschoolers headed straight to the Salvation Army's "angel tree" at the front of the store, where paper angels hung off branches, and each chose an angel. On each angel was a child's name and what they wanted for Christmas: toy trucks, Lego sets, Baby Alive babies. Before they left for Walmart that morning, Muskogee teachers explained to the preschoolers that the kids on the angel tree needed a Christmas gift, and they were there to make sure those kids had something to open on Christmas morning. Then teachers led groups of excited students through the aisles to find the perfect gift for their angel. Muskogee Early Childhood Center calls the event "Attitude of Giving," and for these four year olds, the party is the giving.

All of the kids who toured the aisles of Walmart searching for the perfect gift for their angel come from poverty themselves; 100 percent qualify for the free and reduced lunch program. The preschool, which serves children for only one year at the pre-kindergarten level, provides kindergarten readiness for Muskogee's low-income kids.

Malinda Lindsey, who has run the school for seven years, said that many of her students have typical indicators that they're growing up poor—some have had what are called adverse childhood experiences, or ACEs, like home uncertainty and instability, and domestic violence. Sometimes living in poverty itself can be its own form of trauma. Many face other challenges with social skills such as self-regulation and communication. Many students don't have a place at home to play outside, and probably spend too much time on digital devices. Though these preschoolers already face challenges early in their life, they should still have the opportunity to think of others and practice being good people, Lindsey said. Through a character education program called the Character Education Partnership that Lindsey implemented four years ago, the school is teaching the importance of being a good person no matter what circumstances you come from, and it is doing it to great success.

In 2017, the Character Education Partnership named Muskogee Early Childhood Center a National School of Character, the first school in the state of Oklahoma to be named. Using a framework called the "11 Principles of Character" provided by the Partnership, teachers and administrators weave together moral principles with opportunities for the kids to take action and practice goodness and kindness, like the Attitude of Giving holiday party in the aisles of Walmart. The preschoolers also raise money for kids at St. Jude's, and practice the virtue of gratitude at events like the September 11 commemorative parade downtown, where they thank firefighters, police officers, and first responders for their service while serving them cold drinks.

Lindsey's ideas of intentionally teaching children the benefits of giving are grounded in research. Studies have shown that both talking about giving and role-modeling giving behavior encourages young people to be more generous, and makes them more likely to volunteer. In one study on how parents pass on the value of generosity to their adolescent children, researchers said there was such a strong correlation between both role-modeling and conversation about giving and the rate of adolescent volunteering and giving, practitioners and policy-makers should think about having those conversations earlier to encourage more generous young people.[18]

Showing young people the power of giving to others also encourages love and kindness, two virtues high on the list of importance for parents and teachers. Dr. Thomas Lickona, author of *How to Raise Kind Kids*, wrote that the central question parents can ask themselves is "what kind of person do we want our child to be?" Most parents would say they want their kids to be good people, happy, and successful—but success doesn't mean much without kindness. Lickona said that kindness has three components: "(1) feelings for other people, (2) desire to promote their happiness, and (3) an inner goodness at its source. In other words, kindness is not simply external actions that are helpful, but actions motivated by a certain inner attitude—a concern for another's happiness. Kindness comes from a loving heart."[19]

For Muskogee Early Childhood Center, teaching the value of giving goes beyond formal lessons and trips to Walmart, because Lindsey believes that children learn kindness best when it's shown to them, early and often. That's why the school doesn't even have a suspension rate, and she said she suspends children rarely—and only if absolutely necessary. If children are sent to her for misbehaving, Lindsey often checks to make sure they aren't overtired or feeling unsafe or hungry. She keeps a cot in her office and gives misbehaving kids a chance to rest before addressing bad behavior.

She believes even four year olds aren't too young to understand and internalize lessons about being a good person. "These kids have had 48 months on this earth when they come to us—that's not very long," Lindsey said, "but they're already becoming who they will be. We want to contribute some little pieces for them to be able to live in this democratic world, which is tough when everything is about me, me, me."

"It's really about being respectful," she continues. "How to learn to be kind so that they can make the world more kind. The theory here is that we can teach kids to be more kind. We have an opportunity to form their dispositions and their minds to help them be good learners and dedicated to things and persevere through the tough problems, be agents for change, and peace makers. This is where that learning needs to take place, in these formative years."

THE POWER OF STORY TO SHAPE GOOD CITIZENS

How did General George Washington and the soldiers camped at Valley Forge find it within themselves to face dire circumstances during the brutal January winter of 1777–1778? That fall, the Revolutionary forces had suffered several defeats in battle and were low on food and clothing—they were hungry and cold, without shoes and coats. Disease and death plagued the camps, and the troops were discouraged, disheartened, and ready to give up. What made them push through enduring such misery, when even Washington's faith in victory wavered? It was courage.

Mary Beth Klee believes American courage is something that today's students need to hear more about, a virtue exemplified by so many American heroes—Martin Luther King Jr., Sally Ride, the workers who built the Empire State Building—but often overlooked and undervalued. Klee, a historian and founder of the Core Virtues curriculum, said that too often young students are asked to *analyze* stories such as *Washington at Valley Forge*[20] instead of listening to them and being inspired by them. So she created a curriculum for elementary school children that focuses on telling the stories of virtuous heroes—courageous and diligent, honest and humble, wise and selfless—through the reading of great children's literature. Instead of analyzing, students are asked to emulate heroes with virtuous qualities on the playground, in the classroom, and at home with their families.

"To tell the truth, we're in such a slimy period right now, it's important to put in front of kids the real triumphs of the American story, ways in which we've moved ahead," Klee said about teaching virtue in the twenty-first century. Surrounding young people with stories about heroes, Klee said, can inspire young people to be heroes themselves.

Klee hatched the idea for Core Virtues curriculum more than 20 years ago, searching for a school for her own son in Hanover, New Hampshire, home of Dartmouth College. Klee was concerned at that time with what she saw in local schools as a "values-neutral" approach to character. "It was very, 'let's not dictate morals to anyone, let's let children decide for themselves,'" Klee said. She recalled that "values clarification exercises," in which students practice making value judgments that depend on particular circumstances, were popular. She thought that was a bad idea. "I was looking for something that provided actual guidance for children in terms of character formation."

Inspired by Thomas Lickona's *Educating for Character* and E. D. Hirsch's Core Knowledge curriculum (discussed in chapter 4), Klee wanted to build an orderly, sequenced program to provide missing guidance on character. She wasn't interested in contrived "hokey values tales," but instead wanted something rich and vibrant that young people could get excited about. So she assigned a rotating list of virtues to the months of the school calendar and then layered them through a three-year cycle to be sure no virtue was left behind—from gratitude to generosity, justice to respect, love of country to wonder to stewardship. Through Core Virtues, kids from kindergarten through sixth grade read stories several times a week from a handpicked selection of high-quality literature that reflect the virtue being celebrated that month.

Klee, who eventually opened a school in Hanover that blends the Core Knowledge and Core Virtues sequences, has an English teacher's zeal for the rich language of virtue, and hangs on the words, which do sound—when she says them—like precious gems from an era long forgotten, buried underneath smartphones and cable news, selfies and social media oversharing: *mercy, perseverance, hope.* She makes virtue sound noble, something worthy, to raise yourself up and be better.

Though in today's culture words like mercy and responsibility sound old-fashioned and quasi-religious, Klee said they're neither—they are the common language of human goodness. She said using specific vocabulary and talking to children explicitly, not generally, about how to be good people works. At Crossroads Academy, the school she founded, when children misbehave on the playground, teachers ask them to be more kind or compassionate instead of telling them "that's not appropriate." And Core Virtues schools recognize a child when he or she has been honest, respectful, or generous.

Besides rich language, the Core Virtues schools have another unique trait in character education: a mysterious absence of focus on the self. While other character-building movements focus on the improvement of self—self-esteem, self-awareness, self-management, self-respect—the language of virtue is more focused on how to treat others: with respect, stewardship, charity.

When children learn the stories of how ordinary people behaved in extraordinary ways, Klee said, they begin to internalize these stories and view their own actions through that lens, something sorely needed in the age of the Twitter takedown.

In 2017, the Dalai Lama wrote an op-ed in the *Los Angeles Times* about the need for non-religious ethical education to teach young people the language of a shared humanity. "I see with ever greater clarity that our spiritual well-being depends not on religion, but on our innate human nature—our natural affinity for goodness, compassion, and caring for others. Regardless of whether we belong to a religion, we all have a fundamental and profoundly human wellspring of ethics within ourselves," he wrote. "We need to nurture that shared ethical basis."[21]

MAKING MORAL VIRTUE A WHOLE-SCHOOL EFFORT

"When we look at teaching moral behavior, no one ever said, 'I got to be the way I am from a curriculum," noted Marvin Berkowitz. "Kids get inspired by people. The source of this stuff is from the adults in kids' lives and the social communities they're in who are modeling the behavior." Curricula, he said, can help provide a framework for educators, but in the end raising kids who are moral and kind must be a whole-school, intentional effort to prioritize and reward moral behavior by focusing on the positive, rather than attempting to reduce or eradicate negative behaviors. Instead, promoting well-being, student flourishing, and bringing out the best instead of trying to eradicate a pathology of bad behavior like bullying puts the focus on desired behaviors. "After all, every parent and educator is impacting kids' character right now whether they know it or not. It's just a question of whether they're doing it intentionally," said Berkowitz.

In order to create a school environment that emphasizes civic and moral virtues, Berkowitz said schools should consider the following:

- *Make character an organizational priority.* From classroom climate to the overall school culture, every student and adult should feel like they are members of a community that cares for their well-being and the flourishing of human goodness.
- *Prioritize relationships.* Schools should focus on developing intentional, strategic practices and structures that build positive, healthy relationships, not just between students and between students and adults, but also between adults.
- *Build intrinsic motivation.* Students need to internalize good morals, not just understand them intellectually or know to perform them in front of adults. Knowing how to be good and wanting to be good when no one is looking is the goal.
- *Provide ample modeling of good behavior not just from teachers, but from every adult in the building.* The adult culture in a school sets the tone for the students. Be the character you want to see in the kids.
- *Cultivate student empowerment.* In order to be engaged in democracy, citizens must believe that their voice matters and that others care what they think. Schools should create a democratic environment for students to feel their ideas and thoughts are welcome and invited.
- *Invest in long-term development of character education.* Moral virtues don't appear overnight, and schools should play the long game when it comes to character development instead of focusing on short-term fixes.

FOR TEACHERS TO THINK ABOUT

- Character education is an important topic within the new civics, and falls under social-emotional learning as a "practice to watch" within the proven practices in the *Guardian of Democracy* report (see chapter 1), as plenty of research demonstrates its benefits. Learning and internalizing performance, intelligence, civic, and moral virtues are vital to all of the seven survival skills, from critical thinking to curiosity and imagination, because they are essential to human flourishing.
- In the last few decades, an effort to boost academic performance by teaching and emphasizing performance virtues like "grit" has overshadowed teaching students how to be good people and embody civic and moral virtues, like kindness and caring for the common good.
- Students are never too young to begin learning how to give and care for others, and a moral virtues program is most effective if it is a whole-school effort that includes adult relationships as well.

FOR PARENTS TO THINK ABOUT

- Some young people believe that their parents would rather have successful kids than kind ones. Even though parents may think they are sending the message to their children that they value being good people most of all, that's not what kids are hearing.
- What are the character traits your kids embody that you're most proud of? What are the ones they might need work on? Are they performance virtues, intelligence virtues—or are they civic or moral virtues?
- Research shows that kids who have parents who model giving and caring for others, as well as have conversations about giving and caring, increases the likelihood that their children will do the same.

Chapter Seven

New Civics Innovator

Jack Bradley, "The Rosa Parks of Special Needs Students"

When Jack Bradley was in the third grade, his family was presented with a difficult problem: the school he attended for students with learning differences in his hometown of Louisville, Kentucky, told him they couldn't serve him anymore. Though Jack had been diagnosed with autism, attention deficit hyperactivity disorder (ADHD), Tourette's syndrome, auditory and executive processing disorders, and dysgraphia (a learning disability that makes handwriting difficult), he had scored so high on the math portion of the state standardized test, he no longer qualified for the program. But the truth was that Jack's unique combination of gifts and challenges had made him difficult to serve from the beginning: very early on in his school career, he had been placed in a remedial math class, but his teachers soon learned that he could do the math with ease. He just needed help reading the story problems.

Jack was left without a school that could serve his needs. After months of research and school visits, Jack's mother, Judith Bradley, decided to homeschool him because there wasn't a single school in Louisville, public or private, that was a good fit. Jack is what is often referred to as 2E, or "twice exceptional": he's both challenged and gifted. Jack has an incredible wealth of knowledge and loves learning, but his brain often takes longer to learn new things, called "slow processing." Because of his tics and medications, he tires easily. And the mental and physical effort of handwriting makes taking tests and writing papers exhausting.

In an op-ed on the education blog *Hechinger Report*, Jack explained what his time in school feels like. "A lot of my time in school is wasted—boring and exhausting, organized by skill level instead of by grade. Instead of motivating or inspiring me, it just leaves me feeling exhausted," he wrote. "Please don't listen to my story and think oh, he's just an outlier, because while that's true in some ways, it's not true when it comes to what is most important: I'm just like each of you when it comes to wanting to have friends, wanting to do interesting work and wanting to feel like I'm heard and wanting to enjoy my life."[1]

Jack was homeschooled from third grade all the way through middle school. During that time, he earned a perfect score on the reading portion of the ACT at age fourteen—even though he'd only learned to read four years before. When he rejoined traditional school in ninth grade, he enrolled in two schools, the DuPont Manual High School, a public magnet in Louisville, and the Craft Academy for Excellence in Science and Mathematics at Morehead State University, a dual-enrollment program where he received college credit for his courses.

Now a senior in high school at age 18, Jack and his parents know that his deficiencies come along with some great gifts. His AP U.S. History teacher said Jack could teach parts of the class himself, that's how well he knew the content—yet he needed special accommodations in order to accomplish other tasks like take an exam, which could take Jack up to twice as long as a neurotypical student.

Jack's school experience, in other words, was full of contradictions that made him difficult to categorize, and that was the point of both his and his mother's frustration: in order to reach his potential, he needed more flexibility and freedom. Jack and Judith knew he wasn't the only kid like this, but how could they convince schools that many kids like Jack didn't fit into any category? The only answer, they felt, was to begin telling people what was happening with Jack in school.

Jack's first opportunity to share his experiences took place at the leadership conference of an organization called Best Buddies, which helps to pair those with intellectual and developmental disabilities (IDD) with neurotypical allies in an effort to end the physical, social, and economic isolation those with IDD often suffer. Before he was slated to speak in front of the 20 to 30 people at the conference, he remembered "getting really panicky inside, my heart was beating really fast, and I started freaking out and picturing all the ways it could go wrong."

But once he was given the floor, Jack described for the group what has now become his three-part call for special education reform: first, students like him needed special education teachers with better training, both modernized training in the latest research about autism as well as training on how to help kids with challenging coursework. In addition, general education teachers needed better training on the universal design of flexible learning environments that accommodate students of differing abilities. Second, Jack said students with autism needed more "real-world," intensive social skills therapy. And finally, academic and extracurricular opportunities need to be inclusive of all students, no matter their abilities or disabilities. He envisioned a school environment where there was no "special" or "gifted" education, just an education that suited the needs of every student.

Jack's speech didn't go wrong, as he had worried. In fact, it was so well received that it wasn't long before Jack was asked to speak some more about what was going wrong with special education. And his fear of public speaking slowly subsided—mostly, he said, because he began to feel responsible for making things better for other students.

In 2016, Judith was contacted by college student Andrew Brennan, co-founder of the Student Voice initiative housed inside Kentucky's Prichard Committee for Academic Excellence. After an interview, Brennan asked Jack to join the group, which advocated for students to be more involved in making decisions and governing education in the state of Kentucky. As the first student with disabilities to join, Jack soon began addressing groups of students and educators on behalf of Student Voice.

His anxiety about public speaking was decreasing just as his drive to make change was increasing. He was so driven, Jack said, that he forced himself to do it. His message of reform resonated so much with educators and parents that soon Jack was speaking to larger and larger crowds; in 2018 he spoke to a group of more than 4,000 educators at the education-innovation iNACOL conference about his ideas for school reform. Rachel Belin, director of the Prichard Committee Student Voice Team, called him the "Rosa Parks of special needs students."

Jack's hard work speaking up for special needs students has already brought about changes in Kentucky. Judith has become a full-time advocate for students with special needs and their families, and now serves on two state-level commissions—a parent advisory group with the state's commissioner of education, and Governor Matt Bevin's Employment First Council, addressing education and career opportunities for Kentucky's citizens with disabilities. She created a nonprofit organization, Jack Be Nimble, to help other Kentucky families reimagine special education systems that can work for everyone, and is currently working on legislation that would allow students with special needs to enroll in dual-credit high school and college courses, so they might test the possibility of attending college independently.

Jack said civic activism can be anxious and exhausting work, but he wants to continue because "it's the right thing to do." He wants people to understand that often, someone's struggles aren't happening because of his or her personality, but because of the circumstances. If circumstances can change—if the system around those struggling can change—then the experience can get better. "Clearly communicating with people and being honest with them is, in the long run, much more helpful," Jack said. "One of the biggest problems with humanity as a whole is no one wants to be the first to stand out and make a change. But when one person does speak up, then everyone else feels much more comfortable speaking up. But if everyone's waiting for someone to be the first, then nothing changes. Someone has to start it."

Chapter Eight

Together We Can Do So Much

Revitalizing Communities for the Twenty-First Century

> What the best and wisest parent wants for his child, that must we want for all
> the children of the community. Anything less is unlovely, and left unchecked,
> destroys our democracy.
>
> —John Dewey

When Linda Holloway was a young musician in Denver in the 1980s, she
would often get off work late after playing music in a club, then hop in a car
with her friend Sharon. Together they would head down to Graham, Texas,
to visit Holloway's grandmother, Bessie. Bessie had been diagnosed with
Alzheimer's, and was living in a nursing home. Even though she often didn't
recognize her granddaughter, Holloway still spent days and nights there with
her, talking to her and taking care of her.

But during those visits, Holloway noticed some disturbing aspects of
nursing home life. During the days, most of the nursing home residents rarely
received any visitors. And at night the home was understaffed. Holloway
would wander the dark halls and hear people calling out for help because
they were cold and needed a blanket, or needed assistance going to the
bathroom. The thought that most patients didn't have anyone to visit them, or
help them during the long hours of the night, was unbearable to Holloway, so
soon she and Sharon were bringing Sharon's two young nieces on their late-
night trips to Texas to liven up the patients' lives. During the long daytime
hours, they'd bring their guitars and hold a sing-along in the group meeting
hall. Sharon's nieces would volunteer to be dancing partners with the residents.

Holloway noticed that not only did the elderly residents love the interaction and joy of the sing-alongs—so did Sharon's young nieces. She said it was during one of those afternoons singing and dancing that she stopped and noticed how much the young people and the older people enjoyed each other: the human touch, singing, and fun. She had the idea to contact some school principals in nearby Wichita Falls to see if some of their students might like to visit Bessie's nursing home, to keep the residents company and join in the fun. The schools responded enthusiastically.

Holloway grew an organization out of that experience, Bessie's Hope, that she named after her grandmother, who eventually died from Alzheimer's. Holloway said that Bessie's Hope was "born through" her, and she had a kind of spiritual awakening during the time she spent in the nursing home with Bessie that made her want to help the elderly feel less lonely. Now a large Denver-based nonprofit, Bessie's Hope has been matching young people with elders to form meaningful relationships for more than 20 years, and has served more than 50,000 kids and elders. In addition to the simple joys of companionship, the nonprofit also offers youth programs for service learning, reading groups for struggling young readers, and student-performed living histories—all done with people living inside nursing homes.

Holloway said that she has watched how, for young people, hanging out with the elderly reduces bullying, increases social skills, and helps to develop empathy. She said that the "coming together of old and young people in this meaningful way strengthens the fabric of society, and I believe it has power. It's the only way that our society is going to be saved."

Holloway created Bessie's Hope as an answer to a crisis of loneliness for the elderly, but in the last decade, she's noticed another crisis of loneliness—in the young people coming to visit. She said that the circumstances of modern life make young people vulnerable to the same kind of loneliness she saw in the nursing home all those years ago. Holloway sees loneliness often in young people living in group homes, who've gotten into trouble or been through trauma; sometimes, it's both. She said these teens, many of them boys, often have been reduced to labels like "too hardened" or "too much trouble" to form relationships. But when she gets them involved in the youth-elder activities at a nursing home, routinely a "miracle" occurs. When the boys too hard for a relationship have someone to care about, and someone who cares about them and is happy to see them, they soften.

Holloway recalled one group of boys who were scheduled to visit a nursing home once a month but after several visits, requested they come more often—their elderly friends had told them that they missed them and they were important to them. She said that in the last decade she has found so many young people in great need of finding a community outside their family, friends, and school groups. In her experience, young people are desperate to connect. "Loneliness is an epidemic in our culture . . . it's almost like the older a person gets, the less they are, older means less. And young people are so willing to sit and listen, but we don't take them seriously. So here we have people inside nursing homes and lonely young people outside, both with so much to offer each other."

Even though social media promises instant connection to others through the touch of a button online, Americans are increasingly lonely, and that loneliness affects civic health. In a large 2018 study of 20,000 adults performed by Cigna Health, many Americans signaled that they had few meaningful connections to other humans.[1] To determine how different groups of adults rated their connections, researchers used the 20-question UCLA Loneliness Scale, which has respondents rate the truthfulness of statements like "No one really knows me well," "I feel isolated from others," and "People are around me but not with me," with Never, Rarely, Sometimes, or Often.[2]

The results were staggering: nearly half of respondents reported feeling sometimes or always alone, and slightly more than half said they sometimes or always feel like no one knows them well. Fifty-three percent said they had "meaningful in-person social interactions" daily, like having lunch or a long conversation with a friend—meaning almost half did not have regular interactions with anyone.

Perhaps most surprising of all was that the youngest respondents, those ages 18 to 22 (Generation Z, discussed in chapter 1), reported the highest rates of loneliness. More than half of young people indicated "10 of the 11 feelings associated with loneliness,"[3] and a majority of young people—at a time in life that should be full of connections—reported no one knows them well.

Loneliness doesn't appear to be causing only Americans pain; in early 2018, Great Britain appointed a new "minister of loneliness," the undersecretary for sport and civil society, to tackle their own epidemic levels of loneliness as a health crisis.[4] Though some experts have warned that more data are needed to call this level of reported loneliness a crisis, chronic loneliness is bad for your health and associated with many negative outcomes, ranging from a shorter life span to cancer to suicide.

Why do so many Americans feel so alone? Researchers have been trying to untangle why connections among the most social animals on the planet appear to be dwindling. At the turn of the twenty-first century, sociologist Robert Putnam argued in his book *Bowling Alone: The Collapse and Revival of American Community* that the strong social fabric that gave America its Americanness was fraying. Compiling data from the 1950s through the end of the twentieth century, he showed that Americans were coming together in groups less often. Putnam believed that these associations were crucial to making strong communities and encouraging civic participation.[5]

According to Putnam, who measured every kind of participation from attending PTA meetings to religious services to volunteering for a political party or giving to a charity, Americans in the 1990s were participating far less than they used to a few decades before. Rates of social connection and participation had vastly decreased across all his measures. Even the most casual community connections, like joining a bowling league, had seemed to collapse, as Americans lost what Putnam called "social capital"—valuable networks that connect humans to work, family, and civic life:

> Whereas physical capital refers to physical objects and human capital refers to properties of individuals, social capital refers to connections among individuals—social networks and the norms of reciprocity and trustworthiness that arise from them. In that sense social capital is closely related to what some have called "civic virtue." The difference is that "social capital" calls attention to the fact that civic virtue is most powerful when embedded in a dense network of reciprocal social relations. A society of many virtuous but isolated individuals is not necessarily rich in social capital.[6]

But *Bowling Alone* was written nearly 20 years ago, just as the internet was getting started. The loss of yesterday's social ties may have provided a springboard for today's smartphone-addled society, as Jean Twenge's research on young people, anxiety and depression, and phone usage (discussed in chapter 1) showed that too much time alone with a phone can make teens feel more lonely. Some research disputes Twenge's claims; one study showing that social media actually helps some young people feel less lonely and more connected.[7] And in a national survey by Common Sense Media, a majority of teens reported they believed social media had a neutral effect on their lives, and a quarter said social media helped them to feel less lonely.[8]

Loneliness might not be caused by smartphones, but may be part of a bigger picture—big, fast changes in society as a whole. Sociologist Eric Klinenberg reasoned in a *New York Times* op-ed that though worry over loneliness is a "feature of modern societies,"[9] humans may have just become more individualized over time. He wrote about the modern culture of individualism that has more people living and working alone, exacerbated by the "gig economy" that has many fewer people tied to a long-time place of work. Along with unsteady work, Klinenberg said, a whole host of social connections have been in decline—labor unions, religious services, neighborhood organizations. While Klinenberg doesn't seem to believe that loneliness is an epidemic that needs swift relief, he does emphasize that there is one group of people who tend to be lonelier—underserved and displaced communities—and that there is true cause for concern. In a highly individualized society, those groups are left to fend for themselves and their lives often become highly unstable, making it even more difficult to maintain the connections of a healthy community.

Researchers into civic health look at the problem of loneliness in another way: the communities that underserved and displaced people live in often have few or no opportunities to interact or engage. It's not that people have left their communities; it's that the communities have, in many ways, left them. Researchers have named these communities "civic deserts" because they give citizens relatively few chances to interact with civic institutions and gathering spots. Civic deserts are largely found in rural areas, but can also be found in urban and suburban settings. Weak social and community connections aren't just bad for health outcomes—they're also bad for democracy.

HOW CIVIC DESERTS AFFECT YOUNG PEOPLE

After the divisive 2016 presidential election, researchers at the Center for Information and Research on Civic Learning and Engagement (CIRCLE) at Tufts University, Kei Kawashima-Ginsberg and Felicia Sullivan, wanted to learn more about the stark divisions among the political opinions of young millennials. Using a Tufts study that showed political dividing lines among race, class, and gender, they took notice of one particular divide: rural and urban young people had big differences in political opinions. They wondered how living in a rural area might influence the political involvement and opinions among millennials, and wanted to understand why rural young people may have been attracted to an "outsider" candidate like Donald Trump.

So the two researchers investigated the kinds of opportunities young rural residents had to interact with traditional institutions of civic learning and engagement in their communities. They wanted to see if rural residents had access to places to discuss their political ideas or stay informed about current events within their communities—"places for discussing issues, see various types of leadership and governance structures, addressing problems together, and forming relationships of mutual support."[10] These civic centers could range from civic groups, to preschools (where young people first interact with school as a community institution) and universities, to centers of arts and entertainment, to churches.

What Kawashima-Ginsberg and Sullivan found was that a majority—60 percent—of rural residents under the age of 30 were living in a place with no civic centers, or at the most one.[11] Essentially these rural areas were "civic deserts" without a community base to connect with. And the problem wasn't confined to just rural communities—nearly a third of urban and suburban young people had little to no access to community organizations either (see table 5.1).

In a related study on civic deserts as an American "civic health challenge" published by the National Conference on Citizenship and Tufts University,

Table 8.1.   Access to Institutional Resources by Geography

	Civic desert	Modest access	High access
Urban	29.5%	27.7%	42.7%
Suburban	31.9%	24.8%	43.3%
Rural	59.7%	23.7%	16.7%

Civic desert=0–1 resources, Modest access=2–3 resources, High access=4–5 resources.
Source: Tisch College/CIRCLE Millennial election poll, 2017. Originally published in The Conversation, https://theconversation.com/study-60-percent-of-rural-millennials-lack-access-to-a-political-life-74513.

researchers observed that in addition to a lack of civic community centers as gathering places, there's been a recent, precipitous decline of four big civic institutions that helped to keep communities coming together, staying informed, and addressing community problems: labor unions, religious congregations, daily newspapers, and political parties. Since the 1970s, daily newspaper reading has declined by 50 percent, and regular church attendance and union membership has declined by more than 20 percent.[12]

Kawashima-Ginsberg and Sullivan found that young people who lived in civic deserts were "generally less experienced in civic and political life and largely disengaged from politics; have few, if any, opinions about current affairs; and are less likely to believe that civic engagement like voting and civic institutions—from Congress to local nonprofits—can benefit the community. They were also less likely to help others in informal ways, like helping neighbors and standing up for someone who is being treated unfairly."[13]

Taken together, the decline of civic institutions and absence of organizations keeping people informed, communicating with one another, and helping each other to solve community challenges helps to explain some of the extreme disconnection found in rural communities (and urban and suburban communities as well). The disconnection results in much less civic engagement and participation.

Loneliness, isolation, the rise of individual technology, and lack of access to civic institutions and resources all play a part in why the civic health of communities has deteriorated over the last few decades. These changes should challenge communities, which are the lifeblood of democracy and civic health, to revive and improve the ways citizens can get engaged with one another and participate. Though the days of hashing out a community problem at the bowling league may never be coming back, civic leaders, nonprofit groups, and schools all have the opportunity to rebuild twenty-first-century associations in a way to maximize the potential for today's citizens.

One institution already working to maximize its community potential, working with the changes of the twenty-first century, is the public library.

LIBRARIES AS "PALACES FOR THE PEOPLE"

In the middle of a normal workday morning, the Southeast Branch library in the Antioch neighborhood of Nashville, Tennessee, is full of people and humming with activity. Down the center of the bright, open space are banks of computer stations, nearly every one occupied by patrons browsing the internet, creating resumes, and searching for apartments. Spread across big, brightly colored tables in the corners are English learners and their tutors, quietly repeating their newly acquired phrases.

Moms, dads, and caregivers flip through magazines while their children build Lego towers in the children's section. Retirees drink coffee together in groups at the small café station in the back, having just walked over after working out at the community center next door. And in the back, a mentor gets the teen room ready—the "studio"—for the arrival of all the middle and high schoolers after school, where they will sit and do homework, or hang out, or even work on a new skill like digital sound production or 3D printing.

It's hard to tell from the explosion of life and activity, as well as the floor-to-ceiling windows and modern fixtures, that just a few years ago the library was an empty J. C. Penney department store at the end of an abandoned shopping mall. Once an eyesore, the new library and attached community center have become a center of activity, breathing new life into the neighborhood for Antioch residents.

The library is part of a community effort to revitalize the old Hickory Hollow Mall, which had been closed and empty for years. The city of Nashville took the mall and revamped it as a community space that includes a satellite campus of Nashville State Community College, a brand-new ice rink for public use as well as practice space for the Nashville Predators professional hockey team, a community center with a full workout room and gym, and a 3.5-acre outdoor park. On a warm weekend, the center might be hosting a middle school hockey tournament, a baby shower in the community center, and a yoga class at the library—all at the same time.

Taking a loop around the library and witnessing the different activities by all kinds of people of all ages from all over the world, branch manager Lindsey Patrick said that the library still has books, but they no longer provide the sole source of information—far from it, in fact. The twenty-first-century library provides everything they can to make people's lives better: general education development (GED) classes, yoga, laptops to check out, help with immigration information—all for free. "The library is here to welcome everyone where they are, and provide information. We live in a diverse community and we've got so many people using the library in diverse ways," Patrick said. Long gone are the "shhh" signs; make as much noise as you want—the hub of activity at the library is the "third space," not home and not school, where people can socialize, gather information, and share opinions.

It's also a place where everyone can exist together, side by side, no matter where they come from—a true democratic space at a time when everything from churches to sports arenas to restaurants have become polarized and, to some extent, politicized. The founding principal of the library is "that all people deserve free, open access to our shared culture and heritage, which they can use to any end they see fit," wrote Klinenberg in his book *Palaces for the People*.[14] They're also places of equal and open access to information, a truly American principle.

When Benjamin Franklin opened the first American library in Philadelphia in 1731, books were too expensive for most citizens, and his mission was to get books in the hands of those who couldn't afford them. Franklin later reflected that libraries didn't just make people more intelligent, but served to make better citizens who believed in freedom:

> These Libraries have improved the general Conversation of Americans, made the common Tradesmen and Farmers as intelligent as most Gentlemen from other Countries, and perhaps have contributed in some Degree to the Stand so generally made throughout the Colonies in Defense of their Privileges.[15]

At a time when Americans are sorting themselves into groups in every imaginable cultural space and everything has become commercialized, the library remains a civic institution as well as a cultural one, a true beacon of democracy. But libraries are often ignored as democratic hubs. Klinenberg argues that libraries are undervalued as what he terms "social infrastructure," physical places where social capital (which Putnam described in *Bowling Alone*) is allowed to develop. When social spaces are welcoming and easy to access, "it fosters contact, mutual support, and collaboration among friends and neighbors"[16]—exactly the kind of interaction that young people living in civic deserts need. And when social infrastructure isn't present, the opposite happens: individuals are often left to "fend for themselves," especially dangerous in times of need or crisis.

Social infrastructure is necessary to build the kind of public life and relationships needed to sustain democracy. In order to make decisions about what kind of community to have, citizens within that community need to know one another—and though the neighborhood listserve can provide a digital way of forming relationships, nothing quite replaces the substance of face-to-face interactions. Libraries are a significant place to be intentional about building community, especially in civic deserts.

USING NATURE TO STRENGTHEN COMMUNITY

Ties to community can also be strengthened in another great democratic space: nature. The American ideal of an open, expansive outdoors came directly from the founders, who believed that America should be an "agrarian republic of virtuous citizens who were connected to the country because they worked the soil" and, unlike Europe, "rugged mountains and untamed forest came to represent a country that wanted to see itself as strong and fertile."[17]

Nature provides a free space that belongs to all, where everyone can interact equally. But many kids in Generation Z don't spend time in natural spaces, either because they can't access them, or because parental fears, dangerous neighborhoods, digital devices, and a sedentary lifestyle keeps them indoors.

A few years ago, teacher Sunny Dawn Summers took a group of high school students on a field trip down to the Mississippi River in their home-town of New Orleans, Louisiana. As they stood on the banks that run along-side the city, Summers asked students the name of the enormous body of water they were looking at. Not a single student could name it. "They couldn't tell me what this was called—whether it was fresh water or salt, what direction it was flowing in—nothing," Summers said. "They had no idea they were looking at the Mississippi River, or its impact on their lives." She was "dumbfounded," and realized that students needed to know more about the natural places in which they lived, not only to build communities but to save them from the effects of climate change.

In the fall of 2018 with the backing of a team of designers and an XQ Super School grant, Summers helped found and launch New Harmony High School, devoted to teaching its students, through every subject, about restor-ing and preserving the damaged coastline on which they live. Summers's belief is that citizens can't care for a community they don't know anything about. With their initial freshman class of 45 students, Summers wants to get students into the natural spaces on New Orleans's coastline to learn hands-on how they are interconnected with the land on which they live, and forge deep relationships with the different community organizations working to improve and protect not just the coastline, along with the local people and culture. Much of the student work is project-based, and Summers wants to expose and educate kids about different kinds of social and environmental issues and challenges, hoping they'll find a passion they can study further.

Another name for the work Summers is doing at New Harmony High is place-based education (PBE), a philosophy based on building communities in the natural world. Place-based education has students work on core sub-jects like reading and math through learning and exploring the places where they live, studying local heritage and landscapes. PBE's champion Greg Smith, along with David Sobel, wrote that its chief value is strengthening children's connections to the people and places where they live, and "helps to overcome the alienation and isolation of individuals that have become the hallmarks of modernity."[18]

Place-based education doesn't have to only be about the natural world, but can be a study of all the aspects of a place where citizens live, work, and play, including urban landscapes, architecture, and design thinking. Daniel Rabuzzi wrote:

> "Place" includes "The City," and "your place" embraces a multitude of specific cities, of individual neighborhoods, street corners, pocket parks, the barber shop and the braiding salon, the ball courts, the roti truck and the taqueria, pizza by the slice and a cup of shaved ice, firecrackers and dancing dragons, religious processions, junkanoo and mardi gras, waiting for the bus, street musicians.[19]

Combatting chronic loneliness and the isolation of civic deserts requires community-wide efforts, but place-based education can start building community inside classrooms[20]—often a child's first community. Janis Boulbol and Meg Hopkins, sixth- and fourth-grade teachers in the small town of Sharon, Vermont, have teamed up to introduce place-based education into their classrooms to help bolster a sense of community for their students. Over the last decade the teachers have both watched as more students in their community have been impacted by family trauma like substance abuse and neglect, as well as behavioral and emotional problems. In response, Boulbol and Hopkins created a one-week unit in the nearby woods, studying local plant and animal life and just exploring. They have noticed that the week together in nature calms behavioral issues, and students feel freer.

In the woods, the teachers noticed that students who had the most trouble inside classrooms were often the most curious and the most relaxed. One boy who had been diagnosed with an emotional disorder spent the week digging for animal bones and trying to learn the name of every plant he could without a single emotional incident. Another boy who suffered from neglect at home and was often tuned out and isolated at school found freedom away from class to make friends and be part of the group. The educators worry about the future of kids who are isolated and lonely now, and how that might affect their future civic life. Will kids who feel they don't have a place in the community grow up to become participating members? And will the community be there to support them?

Greg Smith thinks of place-based education as a form of community regeneration, in which its youngest members are shown not just the problems of where they live, but underneath the problems, the possibilities to be built upon. "On the Midwest prairie where the native plants have disappeared, they'll often burn the invasive species, and make it possible for the indigenous plants to return," he said in a phone interview. "All the plants they haven't seen for decades will come back, and it creates this incredible possibility in natural environments for regenerating themselves."

When young people feel a part of their community, they will be more likely to care about what happens there, the kind of "civic disposition" that inspires people to vote, volunteer, and make change. A 2018 NPR story about the struggling indigenous community of Gambel, Alaska, on the Bering Sea related the story of Sam Schimmel. Sam was a teenager who had seen firsthand the generations of community trauma inflicted upon his family's traditional indigenous culture by the government. He grew up with his mother's family, learning the cultural traditions of his heritage: hunting and fishing, as well as learning the traditional songs and stories passed down from his great-grandmother. Over time, Sam's love for his community heritage transformed how he saw the world. As a teen, he became an activist, advocating for Alaskan Native young people, attending the Tribal Nations Conference as a delegate, and representing young people at the Alaska Federation of Natives. He was asked to be part of the Alaska governor's "climate team."

But Sam also credited the strong roots in the culture of his community for saving him from the generations of cultural trauma all around him. "I see that, among my peers, I am much less likely to fall prey to alcoholism and much less likely to be suicidal as a result of being brought up in the laps of my elders, listening to stories and being engaged on a cultural level," he said in the story.[21] "What I've seen is that when youth are not culturally engaged, you see higher rates of incarceration, higher rates of suicide, higher rates of alcoholism, higher rates of drug abuse—all these evils that come in and take the place of culture."

He continues, "It's passing down traditions, stories and ways of life that would otherwise not have a chance to be passed down."

FOR TEACHERS TO THINK ABOUT

- Communities are vital to helping build and develop young citizens, but a large portion of rural, urban, and suburban youth have little or no interaction or experience with civic or community institutions. Without connections to their communities, young people living in "civic deserts" are much less likely to care or be interested in what's happening there. They are also less likely to care about politics, or even helping a neighbor in need.
- Democratic spaces like public libraries provide that community connection for students. They also give young people a chance to interact with diverse groups of people of all ages, races, and cultural backgrounds.

- Place-based education is a way to connect students to their community by teaching them about the natural world they live in or near. Giving young people a sense of place can root them in their community and encourage the students to take care of it.

FOR PARENTS TO THINK ABOUT

- Many young people in Generation Z feel lonely, and believe that no one really knows them or that they have no one to talk to. Helping young people find ways to be connected to their community—whether through religious organizations, the arts, sports, or civic institutions—can help combat loneliness as well as build civic engagement.
- Twenty-first-century public libraries, with their makerspaces, teen rooms, and endless free opportunities to learn new skills, offer an important "third space" for young people outside of home and school. They are great democratic spaces to experience and interact with a diverse group of people.
- Helping young people understand and invest in the local culture of their community helps to develop future citizens who care about what happens in the place where they live.

The chapter title comes from Helen Keller, who said, "Alone we can do so little. Together we can do so much. Only love can break down the walls that stand between us and our happiness."

Chapter Nine

New Civics Innovators

The Young Voices in Newburgh, Indiana

There's a stigma around politics in my own house. At the dinner table we're not allowed to talk about anything controversial, and my parents have told me that if I talked about politics in public, then somebody might disagree with me, and that's rude.

—Elise, age 17, Newburgh, Indiana

On a late Saturday night in February 2018, high school junior Ashton Cady was curled up in her bed in Newburgh, Indiana, scrolling through Twitter in the dark, reading about the latest school shooting at Marjory Stoneman Douglas High School in Parkland, Florida. Her finger clicked on a shaky video of a young girl named Emma González giving an impassioned speech on gun control on the courthouse steps in Fort Lauderdale just days after the massacre.

Cady was transfixed, taken in by González's raw power and charisma and her ability, Cady said, "to get adults to listen." For the past few days, she had been closely following the unfolding events at Parkland from her small suburb on the Ohio River, near the southern tip of Indiana. Though she'd never experienced anything like what González and others were going through, Cady recalled "getting chills" while watching González's passionate plea for change. She had been concerned about school shooters at her own high school for some time, and every time there had been a school shooting somewhere else, she had wanted to do something about it *here*, but wasn't sure exactly what that would be. Watching the video of González changed all that. *Maybe this time talking about guns could be different*, she thought. "If this teenager could make millions of people pay attention to what we have been saying about school safety," Cady said, "then why can't I?"

Then the next Monday, on February 19, Cady's school, Castle High School, received a credible threat of violence via Snapchat and was put on lockdown, in which students go about their normal day with all doors locked and no one enters or exits the building. The school was unsure what could possibly happen, and didn't communicate any information to parents and students; rumors began to fly among students, who were still rattled from the Parkland shooting the week before. They talked fearfully among themselves. Worried parents, nerves still ragged from the 24-hour news cycle about Parkland, rushed up to school to retrieve their kids. Cady's mom decided to come and get her; by the time she left her English class around 10:45, half the school was gone.

No violence occurred at the school that day, or since. But because the lockdown came just days after Parkland, and because there were more school shootings in other American cities in the months to follow, some Castle students felt they were in a near-constant state of high alert and anxiety. Another junior at the time, Jack Brown, remembered feeling raw fear the day of the lockdown, he said he felt like "we were just waiting for something to happen." And for months afterward, the fear continued to rise up daily in this throat when he walked in. "There were days when I came to school and was like, unsure of what was going to happen. It was a really tense environment."

Fear of a shooting at school wasn't students' only concern; some were also having troubles at home. Some of the kids wanted to talk about Parkland at the dinner table, and some were starting to voice political opinions about guns and school—some very different from their parents. In this Rust Belt area of southern Indiana, talking about politics in public was considered rude, and after Parkland, some parents told their children not to talk about gun politics—not at the dinner table, and definitely not at school or in church, or out in public.

Some parents worried that in the polarized political environment, their kids could get in trouble at school, or even hurt, for voicing opinions with which some might disagree. But Cady and Brown, along with a few others, thought that didn't make any sense: why shouldn't they care about issues that are actually happening to them? Emboldened and inspired by González and David Hogg, Cameron Kasky, and Delaney Tarr, Cady and others began asking questions of their parents, their school, and eventually the city council: why don't students have a seat at the school board to discuss school safety and other issues? *Why don't we have a say in how the school gets run?*

So in the weeks after Parkland, a small group of students in southern Indiana had a political awakening and wanted to be heard. Cady, along with another junior named Epiphany Larmey, began spending most days after school trying to find a way to get to Washington, DC, for the March for Our Lives, a gun control march organized by the students from Parkland. After it looked like they weren't going to make it to DC, they had another idea: forming their own March for Our Lives movement at home, in Newburgh.

Larmey asked Amanda Antey, a senior government teacher they had gotten to know because she choreographed the spring musical, to sponsor their club. After much discussion, the students wanted to call it Young Voices, and have it become a place where students could meet and talk about not just gun control, but other social issues that were important to them. Cady said that she and her friends wanted a chance to debate different ideas, and then take action. Antey agreed to sponsor them, since she'd had concerns of her own.

Since the divisive election of 2016, Antey had been concerned about the political "powder keg" between students at Castle High School, exacerbated by the cultural pressure to keep political opinions to themselves. Antey often scanned Twitter in the evenings to read what students were really talking about, and found them enraged, fighting with each other online from after school hours to late in the night. She said the cultural attitude among adults— that talking about issues was somehow unkind or disrespectful—wasn't helping the situation. Teens were living through a complicated time and needed guidance and mentors to learn how to talk about politics; instead, the political silence was doing more harm than good. Political silence was also hurting the civic engagement and responsibility in Evansville and Newburgh, which had already sunk pretty low.

I know more than a little about what it's like to talk politics in southern Indiana, because I grew up in Evansville in the 1980s and early 1990s. The deep roots of the stoic, restrained Germanic culture of the people who settled there in the nineteenth century still influenced public life long after the population became more diverse, and the culture continued to reward political silence and privacy when I was growing up, sometimes above all else. In response to this stifling environment, my father, a middle school social studies teacher, along with my outspoken mother led political and current events discussions at our family dinner table every night for as long as I can remember. But we knew our situation was unusual. I remember friends coming over and being surprised that we were allowed to speak our minds politically, even allowed to disagree with our parents.

But at the top of the twenty-first century, political reticence had somehow turned to disengagement. Voter turnout was abysmal; the average voter rate for all age groups in the Evansville area hovers around 18 percent. This is what worried Antey, and she wanted to encourage her students to become politically engaged, even inviting local candidates running for office to her classroom to talk with students. But she often found that candidates themselves were disengaged from the public, and didn't know about issues important to residents. Some didn't even have websites listing their views and positions on local issues.

Antey hoped that Young Voices could be like a "gateway drug" for civic engagement—drawing in students who wanted to talk about Parkland and gun violence, but then over time more generally addressing civic issues. Perhaps most importantly, she wanted to provide for the teenagers a space to debate and discuss political ideas instead of hurling insults on Twitter. By spring, Young Voices was ready to launch, and on the first Friday meeting 100 students and 10 faculty members showed up. Eli Fanok, a junior at the time who attended the first meeting, said he had been waiting for a long time, long before Parkland set the events in motion, for a place to make a change in his community. "It's not that we didn't want change before," he said. "We just didn't have a place to do it." Antey echoed that sentiment, saying that many students didn't know whom to talk to about their political thoughts, and the group gave them a place to go to express their views without judgment.

Some community adults didn't share the young people's idealism. Young Voices had obtained the blessing of Castle's administration for being a nonpartisan after-school club, and a few months later Cady and a few Young Voices members took their concerns about school gun violence to a meeting of the Evansville City Council. Following remarks on gun control from the local leader of a grassroots group, Moms Demand Action, Cady had the opportunity to speak to the council.

"When I got up to the mic, I tried to say the bare minimum: that as students we don't feel safe in our schools, we'd like some representation and some assurance. And I said that I agreed with Gina [the Moms Demand leader], and I stood with the March for Our Lives movement. That's all I said." One member of the city council began aggressively questioning Cady about gun violence, and quickly indicated that he believed that the blame for gun violence in schools rested with students. "He said that gun violence was our fault because we were bullying kids, and there was a culture of fear in our schools because we put it there. The crowd at the meeting started clapping for him [the council member] while I was up there, and I started crying. It was pretty bad." The interaction caught so much attention, it made the Evansville evening news.

All the contentiousness and the culture of keeping quiet about politics haven't deterred the students, but instead seem to be feeding them a kind of power they didn't know they had. When Cady, Brown, and others returned to school as seniors in the fall of 2018, they began working on a broad, student-centered agenda: starting local chapters of Young Voices at other area high schools and gathering momentum, tackling issues important to them—one of their top priorities for their senior year is improving mental health services in their schools, both related to school safety but also to the quality of their lives in general.

Like many high schools in America, Cady and the other students report high levels of anxiety and depression. "We've been taught to keep it all in. I don't have one friend who is in perfect mental health; we're all kind of stressed and anxious and some are very depressed, and no one's doing anything about it," said Fanok. "School counselors are supposed to be there to help students if they need it, but their time is taken up by all the testing."

Unlike their parents and other community adults around them, the group doesn't seem to be afraid of disagreeing with other students, and Young Voices welcomes all political persuasions. "My whole life I've had beliefs that aren't popular in Evansville, Indiana," Jack Brown said. "But there is room here for plenty of opinions. I don't just want to hear what I want to hear; I want to hear what others think. Then I can learn."

As seniors required to take government, many in the Young Voices group signed up to take Antey's We the People government class, a national curriculum in which they study the Constitution in depth and then compete against other schools. Between We the People class and the Young Voices, the March for Our Lives and the cultural prohibition against talking about politics, the students said they are spending lots of time thinking about democracy and what it means. They are surprisingly optimistic. "In our country it's like we have these two extremes, either yelling and screaming at each other or not talking about it at all," said Brown. "But we just want to express our ideas on how to fix it, that's all we want."

"There's this really strong belief that we as young people can't affect our own future, like we're leaves on the river just being pulled along for whatever happens," said senior Patrick Barner, a self-proclaimed centrist whose father is involved in local politics. "The government is laying the foundation that we are going to have to live in. It's our world; all we want is a voice in our future."

Chapter Ten

A Vaccine against Fake News

Using Less Critical Thinking—Not More—to Protect against Misinformation

On the web, clicks are everything, and entertainment and news are increasingly blurred, material that is sensational, bizarre, or outrageous rises to the top,
along with posts that cynically appeal to the reptilian parts of our brains—to
primitive emotions like fear and hate and anger.
—Michiko Kakutani, *The Death of Truth*

In an ever-changing, incomprehensible world the masses had reached the point
where they would, at the same time, believe everything and nothing, think that
everything was possible and that nothing was true.
—Hannah Arendt, *The Origins of Totalitarianism*

Online encyclopedia *Wikipedia* is the fifth most visited website on the planet,
according to *Wikipedia*,[1] and contains more than 40 million entries in 300
languages, spanning subjects from euthanasia rollercoasters to Watergate,
and everything in between. It's also one of the most maligned websites by
educators, who often tell students not to use it as a source when writing
papers or doing projects. *Wikipedia*'s reputation for being unreliable, that
"anyone" can write the entries or go in and change pieces of information,
harkens back to the website's first days, when the Wild West of the internet
was more open and *Wikipedia*'s entries were easier to change. But that's
really no longer true.

Professor and researcher Sam Wineburg, executive director and founder
of the Stanford History Education Group, said that going to *Wikipedia* for
information is a lot like picking your nose: everybody does it, but no one will
admit to it—but as a source of information (though Wikipedia should be

viewed with caution), the site can be more reliable than people might think. Not just anyone can go onto a page and change it, and have it stick, but depending on the seriousness and popularity of the topic, *Wikipedia* pages have a series of up to 11 or 12 "locks" that protect pages from being edited by anyone but the most experienced *Wikipedia* editors.

There's also a "talk" tab located in the upper-left-hand corner that contains an open, ongoing discussion on ways to improve an entry's accuracy. And at the bottom of each *Wikipedia* page is a series of links intended to support the claims made on each page. But even with all these safeguards, *Wikipedia*'s reputation as a "bad" source of information for students persists. When Wineburg—who has been researching how young people decide what to believe on the internet—asked college freshmen to read two articles on gun control, one from *Wikipedia* and one from a Duke University website, and assess which one was more accurate, most students chose the Duke article as the most reliable—though it turned out to be a thinly veiled polemic coming from the National Rifle Association. The more accurate article came from *Wikipedia*.

Whether we can trust *Wikipedia* as a source of information is symptomatic of something much larger in our all-encompassing online lives, something that twenty-first-century, digitally connected humans deal with every day whether we are aware of it or not: How do we know that what we are reading online is true? Is it fact, spin, opinion—or something much darker? And how do we know for sure? And for parents, teachers, and school leaders—anyone who works with kids, really—how do we possibly begin to teach kids how to tell the difference?

Where does the unending stream of information flowing from the bright little screens in our pockets begin? It can be hard to tell. Articles from the *New York Times* website that have been extensively reported on and fact-checked can appear in the same Google search as a website filled with fabricated conspiracy theories concocted by an anonymous troll. As consumers we are free to click on either or both, in succession, with no filter in between. Though the Russian campaign to intentionally interfere in the 2016 election using misinformation or "fake news" on social media is the most famous and well-publicized example, inaccurate information is everywhere online, extending far out beyond election politics into nearly everything. Widespread misinformation about how vaccines cause autism, for example, spread through social media, have recently resulted in outbreaks of measles and mumps in American cities that eradicated the diseases decades before.

The 2016 election disinformation campaign out of Russia was not an anomaly; research shows that false information used to divide and mislead the public is now a fairly common method of spreading ideas. A 2018 Knight Foundation study of how "fake news" spreads on Twitter found that even though more than 700,000 Twitter accounts were producing false stories just before the 2016 election, they continued to produce fake news long after the election was over. During a 30-day period in March and April 2017, for example, researchers found more than 4 million tweets associated with conspiracy news publishers, and that 80 percent of misinformation accounts remained active well into 2018.[2] Conspiracy sites also might be involved in a plot to misinform the public about the 2020 census: in early 2019, the U.S. Census Bureau asked for help from Facebook, Twitter, and Google to stop the fake news machine from spreading misinformation about who can participate in the census, which could damage the validity of the count.[3]

Even President Donald Trump has jumped on the misinformation bandwagon, turning the term "fake news" on its head and using it to describe articles that criticize him or ones he doesn't like, sowing even more confusion as to what's real. When other world leaders followed suit, news organizations like the BBC warned that the twisting of the term "fake news" had become the "weapon of choice for repressive regimes" and threatened the work journalism does to inform the public.[4]

But beyond the term "fake news," wading deeper into the tangled webs of the internet reveals more subtle misrepresentations that can be just as damaging to public trust. In early 2019, a viral video held the nation's rapt attention for 48 hours. The video, showing teenagers from a Catholic school in Kentucky who were wearing "Make America Great Again" hats appearing to confront a Native American man in Washington, DC, was played hundreds of thousands of times, and shared on social media by news networks as well as individuals. But only after the boys had been excoriated on social media and it was revealed that the Native American had mischaracterized the incident, that footage of the whole video surfaced, providing context and extra information about both the boys and the man that invalidated all the initial judgments about what had happened. While this incident wasn't "fake news" at all—the viral video clip was *real*—the selective cutting and context, along with the thousands of shares, told an incomplete story that led to false conclusions. Yet the damage to the reputations of all involved had already been done.

Humans and democracies need facts and data in order to operate and succeed at any endeavor. From choosing a candidate to vaccinating your children, agreed upon facts are required to make complex decisions that affect individuals and society as a whole. But on the internet facts are becoming more slippery and harder to discern as opinions, and "spin" and downright untruths from unlimited sources on the web overwhelm our information streams and erode trust in institutions once considered trusted sources of important information, like the press. When confusion regarding whom to trust takes over, democracy is in danger, leading to a national social condition researchers call "truth decay"—the diminishing role of facts and analysis in American life.

According to a 2018 report compiled by the nonpartisan research firm RAND Corporation, "truth decay" happens when there is an increasing disagreement over facts and analytical interpretations of facts and data; a blurred line between opinion and fact; an increase in the relative volume of opinion and personal experience compared to fact; and receding trust in institutions once regarded as sources of factual information.[5] Report authors Michael Rich, RAND's CEO, and researcher Jennifer Kavanagh wrote that periods in which misinformation reigned had happened before in our history—the blurred lines of yellow journalism, the radio commentary shows of the 1930s—but they had usually been followed by periods of media and government transparency and accountability.[6]

But the (mis)information age of the twenty-first century might be a bit different. First, the internet isn't going anywhere anytime soon. Instead of two or three or four universal outlets of information, like three major TV networks or the local newspaper, we're now offered an unlimited amount that continues to grow and expand. And when purveyors of information can't agree on facts, they lay claim to their own "alternative facts"[7] and their own interpretation as well, and publish them—where else?—on the internet. In this environment of fuzzy truths, opinions, half-fictions, and downright imaginary stories, readers searching for the facts are left to fend for themselves.

Whether outright conspiracy or more subtle misrepresentation, the news may be fake but the damage—to truth, public trust, democratic institutions, and democracy itself—is real. Misinformation flowing from the internet shows no signs of stopping, and a growing group of researchers, experts, and educators are trying to sound the alarm and figure out how well students fare in this environment of misinformation and "truth decay." Are students able to tell the difference between advertisement and news? Could they properly evaluate a claim made on social media?

YOUNG PEOPLE ARE ESPECIALLY VULNERABLE TO MISINFORMATION

Young people are swimming in information, spending on average nine hours a day online,[8] often with little guidance on what they're reading. (Adults are no better; studies show that adults over 50 actually fare *worse* than young people when it comes to deciphering the difference between fact and fiction on the internet.[9])

Early in 2015, more than a year before the 2016 election and claims of Russian "fake news" interference to influence the American election made worldwide headlines, Sam Wineburg and a group of researchers at the Stanford History Education Group created a set of 56 assessments to measure whether students could asses the credibility of what they were reading online about social and political issues, a skill they termed "civic online reasoning." They distributed the tests to middle schools, high schools, and universities in 12 states, tested wealthy suburban students and poor urban ones, students from highly selective colleges and students from not-so-selective colleges—nearly 8,000 students in all. The results of the test, they found, were "bleak":[10] for a generation of so-called "digital natives" from a variety of backgrounds, many students could not "distinguish between dubious and legitimate sources,"[11] tell the difference between advertising and news stories, or evaluate whether claims made on social media were accurate.

In one test created for middle schoolers, students looked at the homepage of Slate.com, a reputable news and culture site. Students were directed to look at three different items: a banner ad, a news article, and a "native ad," in which an advertisement is made to look like a news article—and then were asked to identify whether each item was an advertisement, and explain why or why not. Though most students (about 75 percent) could correctly identify the news article and the banner ad, they were tripped up by the native ad. The ad's headline, "The Real Reasons Women Go Into Tech," was placed over a newsy-looking photo—even though the words "Sponsored Content" appeared above the headline in large blue print. Eighty percent of middle schoolers responded that the native ad *wasn't* an advertisement.

In another task, high schoolers were shown a photo on the image-sharing website Imgur called "Fukushima Nuclear Flowers." The photo was of distorted-looking daisies that appeared to have overly large, misshapen centers, with a caption above reading "Not much more to say, this is what happens when flowers get nuclear birth defects," referring to the Fukushima Daiichi nuclear disaster. Students were then asked whether the photo and caption "provided strong evidence about the conditions near the Fukushima Daiichi Power Plant." Forty percent of students said that the photo alone, without knowing source of the photo, provided "strong evidence" about conditions near the power plant. Another 25 percent said that the photo didn't provide strong evidence of radiation destruction, but only because it didn't show any other distorted flowers or animals. Only 20 percent of students questioned the source of the photo.[12]

The researchers thought the results of the study might be bad, but were surprised at just *how* bad. Wineburg noted that the quality of information streams is to civics what clean water and air are to public health: democracy can't live without them. The consequences of not tackling the misinformation problem were both unimaginable and at the same time already here: a society that disputes basic facts about social and political issues—rattling confidence, causing citizens to think "there is no truth," giving openings to demagogues—is a society where the very foundations of democracy are at risk. What became clear to the researchers was that most students were using the internet every day, searching for information with no tools to verify that information—the digital equivalent, Wineburg said, of driving on the highway without a license. A driver's license doesn't necessarily indicate that you're an expert about cars, but that you've mastered a few basic skills to keep everyone on the road safe. Wineburg began to think of civic online reasoning in terms of the driver's license analogy, and launched an investigation into how to teach teens the digital version of parallel parking.

IS "MEDIA LITERACY" THE ANSWER?

When Wineburg and the team at the Stanford History Education Group went searching for answers supported by research about what web users do to successfully determine a website's credibility, they came up short. Many of the programs in schools teaching students how to use the internet, often couched under the umbrella term "media literacy," could often include anything from evaluating information to recognizing bias to helping kids combat online bullying and social media aggression.

Media literacy programs specifically aiming to combat misinformation swept into schools around the 2016 election, after an educational panic set in because of "fake news."[13] Resources from nonprofits like the News Literacy Project and for-profit companies like The Day USA offered programs to train students to evaluate sources and recognize bias. A "media literacy week" was established in schools to raise awareness and gain visibility; as of late 2018, advocacy group Media Literacy Now reported that 10 states had either passed or were working on legislation to make media literacy required learning.[14]

Many of these programs designed to combat misinformation for students had a lot in common. They worked generally by giving students a checklist of attributes that they could apply to a website, article, or video when they encountered it to determine its credibility. The lists were created to simplify the goals into something actionable—to "decode media messages, assess the influence of those messages on thoughts, feelings and behaviors, and create media thoughtfully and conscientiously."[15] For example, one poster circulated among educators on Twitter in 2018 instructed young people to "evaluate sources like CARDI B," making an acronym out of the hip-hop star's name. The CARDI B method asked students to notice and ask:

Is the information **C**redible?
Is the information **A**ccurate?
Is the information **R**elevant?
What is the **D**ate when the information was published?
Is the information **I**nteresting?
Is the information **B**iased?

Another popular acronym, CRAAP, asks similar questions to help students evaluate a website's "Currency, Relevance, Authority, Accuracy, and Purpose." For both lists, nested under each question were even more questions that students were supposed to ask themselves to help determine information validity. For example, under "Is the information Accurate?" some questions students are supposed to think about include whether relevant facts can be verified by other sources, and whether there are spelling or grammatical errors on the page.[16]

The idea behind the checklist method was to get students to assess, evaluate, and think critically about what they were seeing on the screen. In this kind of media literacy program, *critical thinking* is the chief skill to be taught—when employing critical thinking, ostensibly students should be able to deconstruct media messages, understand that "seeing is not necessarily believing," and question where the information originated. Students are taught to do this by reading through an article and asking the "CARDI B" questions, as well as employing other guideposts like noticing whether there are banner ads on the website, or whether the article has a date on it.

But the Stanford group wondered whether, when it came to evaluating web information, this kind of critical thinking really worked. To confirm their suspicions, the researchers conducted a study of three different groups who they expected to have a high level of critical thinking and evaluating skills—undergraduates at Stanford, professional historians (who verified sources for a living), and professional fact-checkers—to see whether critical thinking about the information online was the most important skill needed to evaluate the validity of information. What they found was that the critical thinking skills of the Stanford students and the historians paled in comparison to the *verification* skills of the fact-checkers.

Fact-checkers had an orderly, consistent method of verifying web information that didn't require nearly as much "critical thinking" about what they were looking at. Fact-checkers had a completely different approach to the internet in general that allowed them to find information quickly, using a few basic steps. They executed these steps automatically by force of habit.[17] Wineburg had found what he was looking for: the digital version of driver's ed, a few basic skills that anyone could master.

Professional fact-checkers, it turns out, learn the most about a website by leaving it. They don't read web material vertically; they read *laterally*, immediately opening up a series of tabs to scan the rest of the internet for what else has been written about the subject at hand, and put that information into a larger context. Wineburg said that the "web" of the internet is not merely a metaphor—to understand one piece of a web, you must see it in context: fact-checkers treat the internet like an actual web, where everything is connected.

When the researchers gave fact-checkers two articles on bullying, one from the American Academy of Pediatrics and one from the American College of Pediatricians, to determine which article was more reliable, fact-checkers only spent a few seconds scanning the articles, instead searching the web for what else existed online about each group. Wineburg called this "taking bearings," something hikers do:

> Fact checkers' success was closely tied to what we think of as taking bearings, a concept borrowed from the world of navigation. Exploring an unfamiliar forest, experienced hikers know how easy it is to lose their way. Only foolhardy hikers trust their instincts and go traipsing off. Instead they rotate their compass's bezel to determine bearings—the angle, measured in degrees, between North and their desired destination. Obviously, taking bearings on the web is not as precise as measuring an angle in degrees. It begins, however, with a similar premise: When navigating unfamiliar terrain, first gain a sense of direction. [18]

Unlike the historians and students, who took much longer to reach a conclusion and then weren't always correct, 100 percent of the fact-checkers figured out quickly that the American College of Pediatricians was a splinter group with an anti-gay stance, and their bullying article was therefore less reliable. The fact-checkers read less than the historians and the students, but learned more in less time. "They understood the web as a maze filled with trap doors and blind alleys, where things are not always what they seem," the researchers wrote. "Their stance toward the unfamiliar was cautious: while things may be as they seem, in the words of [fact] Checker D, 'I always want to make sure.'" [19]

USING FOUR MOVES INSTEAD OF CRITICAL THINKING

Taking bearings and reading laterally are part of a series of habits that fact-checkers use—the digital version of basic driving skills—to verify web information with speed. Mike Caulfield calls these habits "moves," and thinks they should be taught to all students. Caulfield, who is a professor and the director of Blended and Networked Learning at Washington State University Vancouver, and head of the Digital Polarization Initiative for the American Democracy Project, had been working on his own web literacy curriculum when he was connected with Sam Wineburg, and realized that they were thinking along the same lines. Wineburg helped Caulfield to simplify and hone his ideas on student fact-checking, and from that work Caulfield wrote a book, *Web Literacy for Student Fact-Checkers*,[20] to show teens how to maneuver the web less like CARDI B and more like a professional fact-checker. His four moves to help students evaluate the truth of web information are:

1. *Check for previous work.* Search to see if the claim has already been fact-checked or there's existing research on the topic. For news stories, see what other sources are reporting. For new research, find out what research has said up to now.
2. *Go upstream to the source.* Caulfield points out that most web content isn't original, so heading "upstream" can verify the original source of a claim. This can often be done using hyperlinks within an article that refer back to the original reported information.
3. *Read laterally.* Caufield borrowed Wineburg's term for checking the web like fact-checkers do, putting that information into context about what others say about the source within the wider web. "The truth is in the network," Caulfield wrote.
4. *Circle back.* Another nod to Wineburg; If students find themselves lost or confused, headed down a "rabbit hole" of information, start over. Approach a new search with the knowledge gained from the previous search, and try improving search terms.[21]

Attached to the four moves, Caulfield added one more that he would like students to think of more as a "habit": to check emotions when reading on the web. "When you feel strong emotion—happiness, anger, pride, vindication—and that emotion pushes you to share a 'fact' with others, STOP," he wrote.

> Above all, these are the claims that you must fact-check. Why? Because you're already likely to check things you know are important to get right, and you're predisposed to analyze things that put you an intellectual frame of mind. But things that make you angry or overjoyed, well . . . our record as humans are not good with these things.[22]

Getting the message out to educators and schools about the importance of fact-checking and the "four moves" is an urgent priority for both Wineburg and Caulfield, and both are working to expand their reach. Caulfield's book is being picked up by librarians around the world. Wineburg has joined forces with Google, the Poynter Institute, and young adult author John Green to create the MediaWise project, aimed at getting the fact-checking curriculum spread to middle and high school students, especially ones from underserved communities. A small pilot study to test the fact-checking curriculum for college freshmen, about 150 minutes' worth administered over a 15-week semester, showed demonstrable improvement[23]—but Wineburg said it's not enough. He hopes that in a decade, fact-checking lessons will be a given to every student, using his "driver's license" approach to the internet: knowing the basic rules of the road.

Wineburg is confident that schools will eventually catch up; he said that after the 1950s "Sputnik moment," schools retooled their curriculum to beef up STEM programs, and he thinks the same will eventually happen with civic online reasoning. The only difference is what's at risk.

"What's at stake here is liberal democracy," he said. "We're faced every day with social media posts and stories that inflame emotions and extinguish our ability to rationally think. Liberal democracy teaches people to look at the evidence and make a thoughtful decision based on reason, rather than fear."

FOR CIVICS, A QUESTION OF TRUTH

Teaching civic online reasoning to students isn't just a much-needed, twenty-first-century civics lesson: truth distortion on the internet has real and dire consequences. As an example, in the span of a few weeks in late 2018, three separate incidents of online misinformation made national headlines: a CNN video of a presidential press conference scuffle was doctored and re-released by the White House to present a preferred version of the truth; midterm election recounts provoked lawsuits and accusations of fraud that spread on Twitter and quickly turned to conspiracy theories, taking on the characteristics of an old-fashioned child's game of "telephone." And most tragically, an anti-Semitic man who had been radicalized online on a far-right social networking site attacked a synagogue in Pittsburgh and murdered 11 members. In each incident, digging out the facts of what happened isn't just good to know, but crucial to democracy.

Michiko Kakutani wrote in her book *The Death of Truth* that the foundation of democracy rests on the truth: "'We the people' can't vote for candidates or reach consensus on what should be done when we each have our own version of the truth. We've become so polarized, Red America and Blue America can't even agree on the same facts, each group siloed into our own 'bubbles' through algorithms and social media echo chambers that reinforce our beliefs."[24]

Caulfield said that in his interactions with college students, what concerns him most is not that they're so gullible and prone to believe anything they read on the internet. In an environment of "fake news" and misinformation, instead many cynically believe that nothing is really true. "With information overload, what we see happening is that students have low trust in everything. They don't know how to sort true from false in an effective and efficient way, so their defensive strategy is to more or less trust nothing. It's called trust compression, where you don't really find things that you trust highly, your trust is compressed between low and slightly less low. Show them a prompt from a reputable newspaper and something fake, and it's low trust for the truthfulness of both, across the board."

Caulfield is insistent, like Wineburg, that when it comes to the internet, critical thinking will *not* solve the truth problem of who and what to believe. Critical thinking skills, which include being able to reason, evaluate evidence, and deduce conclusions about information, can't be used when reading a web article on topics students don't know anything about, like nuclear science or immigration law—because students often don't have the most basic knowledge, much less expertise in the topic to even begin to employ critical thinking about whether or not it could be accurate. A better idea, Caulfield said, is for students to know how to figure out who is an expert in nuclear science, or immigration law—and whether or not they can be trusted to tell the truth.

Some research even suggests that conspiracy theorists are actually practicing high levels of critical thinking. "In one sense, conspiracy theorists are really good critical thinkers," Caulfield said. "They're just applying that skill to a mountain of so-called 'evidence' that they should be discarding. Applying critical thinking to garbage doesn't work. That's why before you think critically, go and filter and sort what you're looking at. Make sure it's worth thinking about."

At the close of *The Death of Truth*, Kakutani quotes Jefferson on the importance of reason and truth to uphold the republic: "I hold it therefore certain that to open the doors of truth, and to fortify the habit of testing everything by reason, are the most effectual manacles we can rivet on the hands of our successors to prevent their manacling the people with their own consent." During an era of fake news, election hacking, and political polarization, using civic online reasoning to help students wade through misinformation and disinformation on the web is critical to the future of democracy. But Wineburg, Caulfield, and others stress that online reasoning shouldn't be limited to just civics or politics, but a given part of every classroom subject, including science and math. The more students practice with the precision of fact-checkers, the more adept they will become at being able to burrow out the truth.

FOR TEACHERS TO THINK ABOUT

• Media literacy, critical online reasoning, and teaching students how to assess the truthfulness of what they read online is a crucial part of the new civics. Media literacy was recently added as a "practice to watch" within the *Guardian of Democracy*'s proven practices (see chapter 1), and research shows that students can't tell the difference between fact and fiction. Media literacy education incorporates several of the seven survival skills for the twenty-first century, including analyzing information and problem solving/critical thinking.

- According to Wineburg and Caulfield, students need a simple set of habits, not long checklists, to quickly evaluate whether online information is accurate. Just like learning to drive, students need to use less critical thinking, not more, when they are navigating information online, and need to behave more like professional fact-checkers.
- Media literacy education is an urgent need, as nearly every student receives news through online sources, and learning to evaluate accuracy is crucial to civic health.

FOR PARENTS TO THINK ABOUT

- Media literacy is as important for adults as it is for kids. Do you know how to make sure an online source is telling you the truth? Learn the fact-checker's quick rules and model them for your kids.
- Young people need to be reminded early and often that just because it appears on the internet or in their social media feed doesn't mean it's true. Talk to kids about how to investigate the truth of claims made online, and show them how to check and see whether a source is reliable.
- Have you ever shared something online that turned out to be bogus? Share those experiences with your kids, and explain how easy it is to be fooled.

Chapter Eleven

New Civics Innovator

The Accidental Activist

Shishmaref, Alaska, is a city literally falling into the sea. Nathan Baring, age 18, lives more than 500 miles away in Fairbanks, but has friends in the indigenous Inupiat coastal village near the Arctic Circle, and he has heard firsthand stories about how climate change is forcing the citizens to move. Because sea ice is no longer forming each September like it did for centuries or perhaps even millennia, the coast can no longer protect itself from the Bering Sea's violent winter storms. Waves that used to crash into a solid wall of sea ice are now folding themselves directly onto the coast of the tiny island, dragging the coastland back into the ocean.

It's not just Shishmaref; the whole of Alaska is seeing the effects of climate change. Baring—who speaks in a measured, mature way that makes him sound much older than he is—said everyone in Alaska knows climate change is real, you'd have to be blind or simply never step foot outside to think otherwise. And he's been trying to alert the public and the government about the potentially disastrous effects of the rapidly warming Arctic since he was 13 years old.

Baring, a high school senior and self-described "climate-change geek" who projects both pragmatic detachment and deep passion, spends lots of his free time outside of school learning more about climate change, attending lectures and public events at places like the Climate Change Research Group in the International Arctic Research Center at the University of Alaska Fairbanks, just blocks from his home, to learn more about what will happen to Alaska when the permafrost thaws, the glaciers melt, and the homes along the coastline disappear. He's constantly educating himself, reading books and the local paper, the *Fairbanks Daily News-Miner*, and talking with experts as much as he can.

Once Baring knew the facts about how devastating climate change will be to his home state, he felt he had to do something—anything—to try and save it. "I tried every single avenue of civic discourse you can think of," Baring remembers. "Organizing, marching in the street, writing letters to each of my members of congress, lobbying local legislators in Juneau, petitioning, writing letters to the editor galore—I wrote my first letter to the editor about climate change in 2013, when I was 13 years old."

None of his civic engagement seemed to solve the problem; politicians and the public weren't listening, and Baring watched in frustration as Alaska continued to get warmer. And warmer still. Oil revenues, on which Alaska depends as a major contributor to its tax base and workforce economy, weren't helping but instead making things more complicated—how can Alaska stop climate change and keep drilling oil at the same time?

In 2015, when Baring was 15, he traveled to Juneau to attend the Civics and Conservation Summit for the nonprofit Alaska Youth for Environmental Action, where he learned how to take his passion for climate change to the next level. Along with other teens, he met legislators and learned how to advocate for the climate, and how the democratic process works. But nothing ever came of his work there, and Baring went home.

Then a few months later, Alaska Youth for Environmental Action reached out to see if he was interested in joining a lawsuit of young people across the country suing the U.S. government for knowingly taking actions that destabilized the climate, caused climate change, and threatened their future. Baring said he knew immediately that he wanted to join the lawsuit; all the other civic tactics he'd tried to change the conversation on climate change had failed.

With the help of an Oregon nonprofit called Our Children's Trust organizing the lawsuit, in August 2015 Baring filed his declarations along with 20 other youth plaintiffs from 11 states, including Oregon, Colorado, Hawaii, Florida, and Louisiana, under the lawsuit *Juliana v. the United States*. The lawsuit claims that the plaintiffs' constitutional right to clean air and water, and their right to enjoy a stable climate and secure that climate for future generations, are being violated by the extraction of fossil fuels. It also argues—using the Public Trust Doctrine—that a stable climate capable of sustaining human life is a public resource that should be protected by the government.

At first the fossil fuel industry intervened and joined the U.S. government as defendants in an attempt to dismiss the case, but it failed. Through 2016 and 2017, the case weaved its way through district courts, finally landing in the Ninth Circuit Court of Appeals in July 2017. By that time, the Trump administration had filed its own petition to have the lawsuit dismissed; after hearing responses from both district courts and the youth plaintiffs on the proposed dismissal, in March 2018 the Ninth Circuit rejected the petition for dismissal and granted the lawsuit to proceed.

By July, the Trump administration's application had made its way to the Supreme Court, which ruled unanimously in favor of the young people's right to go to trial. As of late 2018, the young people, many now in their early 20s, were finally set to go to trial against the government on October 29. If they won, they would ask the government to put in place a national climate recovery plan that returns greenhouse gases to acceptable levels, at 350 parts per million, by 2100.

In September 2018 Baring left Fairbanks for his freshman year of college at Gustavus Adolphus College in St. Peter, Minnesota, to study political science and biology, and prearranged his schedule to be able to take time off in order to attend the trial. But there isn't much chance he will make a career out of being an activist for climate change. Though Baring had been actively trying to work against climate change for more than six years, since he was in junior high, he's never been comfortable with the word "activist" and bristles at the term.

He said that some of the other plaintiffs, like the hip-hop artist and activist Xiuhtezcatl Tonatiuh Martinez, have activism in their bones, come from "hippie families" in Oregon and Colorado, and have grown up surrounded by environmental activists, while Baring has not. His mother is a school nurse and his father is an elementary school teacher. Baring sees his activism as temporary, as trying to solve a problem that deeply worries him—more of an "interested citizen" looking to solve a single problem. And he hopes that after the lawsuit is over, and after they win (he remains seriously hopeful), he can "vanish in the shadows of a career that I care about," and live a "normal" life. He worries that in the twenty-first-century's volatile political atmosphere, other young citizens like him see activism as a job, a career choice, and Baring thinks that should change.

"I don't believe anyone should be an activist as a career," he said. "To me, one of the problems with 'low civic engagement' is that people expect the 'activists' to take care of all these problems because that's their job. A successful republic requires that sometimes people have to be willing to set aside some of their own lives when a true injustice arises. I saw human-caused climate change, furthered by the actions of our government, as a great injustice that will befall my generation, and I had to be willing to step outside of my comfort zone to work on correcting it.

Baring continues, "I know there are millions who feel the same way, and I think the recent groundswells of public support for global climate action are what may allow us to finally turn the tide."

Chapter Twelve

Learning How to Talk and Listen

Civil Discourse in a Polarized Age

America doesn't just have arguments; America is an argument—between Federalist and Anti-Federalist world views, strong national government and local control, liberty and equality, individual rights and collective responsibility, color-blindness and color-consciousness, Pluribus and Unum.

—Eric Liu

Amanda Smithfield has been a high school educator for more than 20 years and understands that any good discussion begins with two things: preparation and pizza. On a warm October day, kids rushed into Smithfield's library during their lunch period at Hume-Fogg Academic Magnet High School in downtown Nashville, Tennessee, grabbed a slice of cheese or pepperoni, and sat down to prepare for an informal discussion on whether or not Brett Kavanaugh should have been confirmed to the Supreme Court.

As about 50 kids wound their way to pre-assigned tables—to ensure each small group was a healthy mix of both left-leaning and right-leaning views—Smithfield clipped a microphone to her shirt and, over the shuffling noise of backpack-arranging and pizza-chewing, reviewed the rules of the day: listen carefully to what others are saying, even if you disagree, and make sure your response reflects that you heard and understood them. Be courteous and don't interrupt. Support your arguments using evidence. Avoid inflammatory language and speculation. Criticize the argument, not the person. And most of all, respect others' rights to hold opinions and beliefs that differ from your own—in other words, the opposite of every Facebook argument you've ever had.

"So really what we're doing today is celebrating the First Amendment. What are the five freedoms guaranteed to us by the First Amendment?"

Smithfield asked. Kids shouted them out—religion, press, speech, assembly, petition—as Smithfield counted them, in the air, on her fingers. "We should be cognizant of the fact that we are really lucky to have the freedom to talk about this issue today. And if you don't like what someone says today, you disagree with them—then guess what? You've got freedom of assembly, you can go out and advocate for whatever it is you think is right."

In case the spirit moved them, Smithfield had placed a sample letter addressing their district's congressman on each table, complete with his address. Then Smithfield made a little waving gesture with her hand to signal "let's get started"—the October meeting of Smithfield's lunchtime project to improve democracy, which she has named Project Civility America, had begun.

Questions had been placed at each table to help guide a discussion that had recently roiled and divided the entire nation, and Smithfield worried it might get emotional. Weeks after Brett Kavanaugh was nominated to the highest court in the land, a California professor named Dr. Christine Blasey-Ford had come forward and accused Kavanaugh of sexually assaulting her when they were both teenagers. The accusation, which came on the heels of other assault accusations by women of powerful men, like film producer Harvey Weinstein and President Donald Trump, were part of the national #MeToo movement, and seemed to tear an already divided nation into two passionate groups—those who believed that the accusation alone was enough to prevent Kavanaugh's confirmation to the Supreme Court, and those who didn't.

Students had been asked to read two articles the night before, one supporting Kavanaugh's nomination and one against it. At one table, a conservative-leaning senior sat with two liberal sophomores and a freshman, and said she was still undecided. Yet they dove into the conversation without any hesitation or shyness, starting with the testimony of the accuser, Blasey-Ford, followed by details of Kavanaugh's conflicting testimony.

One of the table's freshman, named Sam, said that it was unfair to give the Senate only a week to investigate Blasey-Ford's claims. "They needed more time to investigate, rather than a week, though I guess the Senate is majority Republican and they're not going to change their minds anyway."

Then Rachel Harrington, the conservative senior, said, "I do think that Kavanaugh should have been confirmed, because there is such a lack of evidence. There are big holes in both testimonies. If they could prove that this happened, then ok. But they couldn't. If he was qualified before, then he should be confirmed."

Rose, a 15-year-old sophomore, admitted that she still couldn't firmly form an opinion. "I'm kind of undecided," she said. "If they took back his nomination and it turns out that he didn't assault her, then his reputation would be ruined for no reason. But if it could be confirmed that he did it, should he be seated? I don't think so."

But soon the teens moved on to bigger questions, like whether the investigation had been thorough enough, and how to balance believing survivors of assault with "innocent until proven guilty." Students were careful to support their arguments with what they had seen or read in the news. They seemed to take Smithfield's suggestion that they listen first with great seriousness, allowing anyone who was talking to finish what he or she had to say before adding or disagreeing; sitting face to face, students also seemed to agree on certain aspects of highly polarizing ideas about survivors or sexual assault in ways one would never experience on social media.

Teens who regularly attend Project Civility America—also known as Project Civ—enjoy it. Rachel Harrington, the senior lone conservative at her table, said she doesn't just like Project Civ, she loves it, and never misses a lunchtime meeting if she can help it. Harrington said she only knows a few students at Hume-Fogg who are politically conservative, and was tired of having arguments in the hallway over gun violence or any other issue in the news. "Hume-Fogg is very diverse in a lot of ways," Harrington said, referring to the magnet school's pull from all of Nashville's neighborhoods, "but we don't have viewpoint diversity."

At a table at Project Civ, she can share her views but also get details of why progressives think what they think. She said that she has changed her mind about topics based on what she learned at Project Civ, too; her stance on DACA (Deferred Action for Childhood Arrivals) changed once another student explained to her that young people living under DACA didn't choose to come to the United States. Now she supports citizenship for DACA students.

And she has persuaded others to her way of thinking as well. "Last year, in a discussion on gun control, I was talking about how I think that when it comes to mass shootings the problem isn't guns. When my parents were in high school, kids came to school with gun racks on their trucks, but no one ever shot anybody," Harrington said. "I think the problem is mental health issues. And there was this girl, a sophomore, who said, 'Hey maybe Rachel's got a point.' This made me happy, it was like, hey, somebody is actually seeing my side of it this time."

Sophomore Katie Madole often sits at the same table as Rachel Harrington, and doesn't often agree with her on issues like gun control and immigration. But she thinks Rachel is great, and loves to sit at her table—every time she does, Madole said, she learns something. Madole rarely misses a meeting and is proud to say that because of what she's learned at Project Civ, she's no longer afraid to say to someone, "I politely disagree." She even took her new skill to her summer Girl Scout camp, where she noticed a planned discussion on gun control caused a lot of the other girls to clam up, afraid to say what they really thought. Madole ended up coaching them in the way Ms. Smithfield coached her. "Don't be scared to disagree with me," she told the other scouts. "Don't be scared to tell me I'm wrong!"

Like looking in a rearview mirror, Smithfield believes that polarized Americans' opinions about what's best for the country are closer than they appear—they just have different ideas of how to get there. Project Civ is a professional and personal project for her, a place to channel all her seemingly bottomless enthusiasm for young people discovering the beauty of the link between disagreement and democracy.

Smithfield has been gathering groups of teenagers in the library to use civility in discussing hot-button issues once a month since March 2018, when the massacre at Marjory Stoneman Douglas High School in February, and the ensuing youth protests and walkouts, made her realize that the young people inside her school needed a place to talk and learn about the issues and have a place to work out their thoughts on them. Mostly, she was worried that the voices of the conservative students at Hume-Fogg, who are in the minority in the mostly left-leaning school, would be drowned out in the ongoing conversation on gun violence and gun control.

Earlier in the year, some students had come to the library to print out tickets to attend a Trump rally happening in downtown Nashville, and Smithfield said they were shy and almost embarrassed to ask her to print them— that's when she realized that they didn't have opportunities to voice their political opinions at school. "I told them, of course I'll print them, and I'm so glad you are doing this. Any time you have the opportunity to see the President of the United States speak, you are participating in the political process, and that's great." Smithfield told them she might see them at the rally, as she would be outside, observing the protesters. "I really respect the kids, and they respect me, and I want to be encouraging. I'm willing to be an advocate for students no matter what their political beliefs are."

Though she'd had her eye on a civility project since the 2016 election, after the spate of school shootings, Smithfield said she saw how political polarization over topics like school shootings could become a danger to their school community and democracy at large. As a librarian and the sponsor of both the high school Democrat and Republican after-school clubs, Smithfield thought the library would be the perfect place to hold "normed" discussions and give students practice on how to have civil discussions on hot-button and controversial topics—not debates. "Debate suggests that there is going to be a winner and a loser, and that's not what we're doing here. We're having a conversation and giving everyone a chance to hear and consider opinions that are different from their own. We're here to learn."

AMERICANS NEED BETTER ARGUMENTS

Smithfield's plan to get young people practicing how to disagree reflects a larger national conversation about how Americans can talk to each other about complex issues without losing their minds. Recent research shows that the farther Americans wade into the twenty-first century, the less we seem to agree on. A Pew Research study from 2017 showed that over the last two decades, Americans have siloed themselves by political belief, and fewer and fewer Americans hold a mix of conservative and liberal views. In 1994, 49 percent of Americans' beliefs were an equal mix of right and left. But by 2017, that number was down to 32 percent.[1] In a related study, Pew found that half of Republicans and 46 percent of Democrats could at least agree on one thing: talking politics with those they disagreed with was "stressful and frustrating" instead of "interesting and informative."[2]

But focusing on coming to a final agreement on what to do about gun violence, climate change, or immigration might be looking at partisan issues the wrong way; what if the push and pull of argument is what makes our democracy vibrant and alive? That's the argument put forth by a national civics initiative, the Better Arguments Project: Americans might find common ground if they did less yelling and dismissing and more listening.

The concept for Better Arguments was outlined by Citizen University founder and author Eric Liu in an article for the *Atlantic*: polarization hurts and everyone feels bad about it, but that doesn't mean Americans should rush to repair the rift without first examining what exactly it is each side is arguing for. In order to work out the differences between deeply entrenched tribes with strong beliefs, there must be a reckoning before reconciliation, and reckoning in this case would mean "naming the inherited power inequities that have brought us our contemporary conflicts. This is the 'truth' part of 'truth and reconciliation.'" Only then, Liu wrote, can true unity and civility return.[3]

If there is to be the kind of reckoning Liu describes, then left and right will require *more* arguing, not less—a necessity in order to heal. So better arguments are in order, but often people don't know what those look like. In a 2018 report, *What Is a Better Argument?* a team from the Aspen Institute of Citizenship and American Identity and the education organization Facing History and Ourselves interviewed more than 75 experts to formulate how Americans could argue—with civility and respect—their way out of the stark polarization that plagues the nation. Their five principles of a better argument[4] include:

1. *No winners, no losers—only listeners.* A better argument prizes listening, not earning points for disputing the opposition's claim. Instead of

looking to win, arguers should join in a common, community-building goal of seeking out the truth.

2. *Relationships trump being right.* People who care about each other in positive relationships are more likely to listen, and "when relationships are adversarial, arguments often lead to more polarization." Adversarial relationships should focus on changing the nature of the relationship to something more collaborative; then the relationship becomes more important than the argument.

3. *Context matters.* Discussions don't happen in a vacuum; what are the concerns and culture of the particular groups locked in disagreement? Discussions that happen within communities should always focus on the needs and issues of that particular group instead of highlighting wider, vaguer tensions.

4. *Trust leads to vulnerability.* One reason Americans only engage with their "side" is because it's safer. Better arguments happen when an environment of trust enables participants to make themselves vulnerable—and vulnerability can often lead to finding areas of agreement. Exercises that establish a group's commonality and humanity—often using humor and personal stories—can build trust.

5. *Engaging leads to transformation.* Once winning and resolution are no longer goals, arguments can focus on listening to those you disagree with and building community, and that can be an inspirational and transformational experience.

Young people studying civics can—and should—learn to have better arguments, too, though teens are often discouraged from participating in political discussions because it's assumed they're not knowledgeable enough, or should be protected from the adult world of hateful politics. After a white supremacist rally turned to riots and the death of Heather Heyer in Charlottesville, Virginia, in 2017, school counselor Terri Tchorzynski of Battle Creek, Michigan, commented, "Our society tries to shield difficult conversations and horrific events from our youth because it is assumed that they don't understand what is going on, or that they are too young to be exposed to some harsh realities. But the reality is that our young students are hearing about these events and developing their own opinions—sometimes with some lack of knowledge or guidance."[5]

For many young people interviewed for this book, discussing politics wasn't an option at school or at home. Many teens expressed a desire to test and work out their political thoughts and beliefs, but were told by adults that they shouldn't speak out, or that it was rude to talk politics and might offend a friend or family member. Other adults worried that young people arguing about politics would cause fights. But what would happen if young people had a chance to practice having political, issue-based arguments guided by knowledgeable adults? Two educational researchers have found that when young people have the kind of better arguments Eric Liu prescribes and Amanda Smithfield is practicing at Project Civ, they learn not just about politics, but about what it means to live in a democracy.

A TWENTY-FIRST-CENTURY GUIDE TO POLITICS
IN THE CLASSROOM

Students like Rachel Harrington and Katie Madole who participate in political discussions about controversial topics led by a knowledgeable teacher find them highly engaging and learn a lot from them—but not many American students get that opportunity. Research consistently shows that students who engage in the most classroom discussion are often on higher academic tracks as well as socioeconomically advantaged,[6] creating an opportunity gap for practicing the kind of deliberation of difficult topics that researchers say is an education on how to live and practice democracy.

In a four-year study of classroom political discussions between 2005 and 2009, Diana Hess, dean of University of Wisconsin–Madison's School of Education, and Paula McAvoy, assistant professor of Social Studies Education at the North Carolina State University, set out to examine what students learned from classroom political discussions, and whether those experiences influenced their future civic engagement and behavior. In addition, they wanted to study the teachers providing the "high quality" discussions to find out what they were doing right.

In their book about the research, *The Political Classroom*, Hess and McAvoy argue that schools, in order to fulfill their democratic mission, should be political (though not partisan). Political classrooms "seek to teach young people to see each other as political equals and to inculcate them into the practice of reason-giving and considering how their views and behaviors affect others."[7] In political classrooms, students learn how to discuss topics that have multiple, competing views, and practice listening and questioning.

Creating the kind of political classrooms and democratic education that students need has always been difficult, but is now even more so in our current highly polarized climate. McAvoy and Hess note that often teachers choose to avoid having political discussions in classes that are teaching the lessons of politics (like history, government, and civics) because facilitating talks about controversial topics is full of pedagogical challenges—navigating students' family cultural and religious values, the polarized political climate outside of school, and the fear of parent backlash all make creating a positive environment for political discussions much more difficult.

Teachers are also wary—rightfully—of how their attitudes and personal opinions can influence the developing ideas of impressionable young people, and must also be aware that students have more first amendment rights to free speech than they do as state employees. "Teachers are in a position of authority and can dramatically affect the life prospects of students [who] understandably will self-censor to avoid offending the person who controls their grade," wrote political science professor Joshua Dunn at University of Colorado Colorado Springs in the upcoming essay collection *Talking Out of Turn: Teacher Speech for Hire.*[8] All around, classroom political discussions can be fraught with minefields.

But that shouldn't discourage teachers from holding political discussions in class. When done well, Hess and McAvoy argue, allowing students to talk to each other about controversial topics has the potential to increase civic knowledge, skills, and dispositions that lead to adult civic engagement. The key to creating a positive environment for discussion, they found, was guidance by a well-prepared and knowledgeable teacher.

Best Practice Educators

To find out what was happening inside classrooms where students learned the most from discussing controversial topics, McAvoy and Hess studied the work of 35 social studies, history, and government educators, some that used curriculum that focused on deliberation of controversial political issues and some that taught lecture style. Then they compared the two types of teachers to see how they engaged students and what students learned.

All of the teachers they studied had quite a bit of teaching experience, and the majority had degrees in history or political science. Out of this group, the researchers found 10 to 12 teachers they labeled "Best Practice teachers," who conducted political discussions where students learned a lot and later showed indications of increased civic knowledge and engagement. These Best Practice educators held discussions of controversial topics at least once a week in class, were all politically aware and engaged themselves, and often shared that knowledge and enthusiasm with their students.

McAvoy said in an interview that Best Practice teachers also had a lot of support and professional development to learn how to conduct classroom political discussions. Teachers sometime assume, McAvoy said, that classroom discussions don't require much preparation upfront, but the opposite is true. Good discussions have lots of upfront preparation, including the teacher creating discussable questions, students reading something in advance, incorporating discussions into a unit of study, and educators making sure that students are talking to each other, not the teacher.

Surprise discussions sprung on students can go off the rails quickly. "If the Monday morning after the Charlottesville riots a teacher just walks into her classroom and asks the students, 'Well, what did you guys think of that?' That's going to be a disaster," McAvoy said. An open discussion right after a tragic event, with questions like "how do you feel about this situation?" or "do you have questions?" allows students to process—but it's not the time to debate free speech, or what to do about monuments. "If you let kids just shoot from the hip, it will be divisive and will allow students to just state their biases and their prejudices without any guidance," McAvoy notes. Using discussion strategies like role-playing, supporting statements with text and research, and student understanding of knowing how and when they are supposed to participate will make a discussion more productive and effective.

Best Practice teachers also know how to push student thinking, especially if, like many American schools today that are "sorted" into more like-minded groups, the class mostly agrees with one another on certain topics. In their book, McAvoy and Hess describe how social studies teacher Joel Kushner at Academy High School plays "devil's advocate" to his left-leaning students on topics like abortion, trying to nudge them to understand the pro-life point of view and see there are reasonable competing ideas on both sides of the issue. Kushner said,

> With abortion, I try to make the arguments as best I can. I divide it up: today is the pro-choice view, today is the pro-life view, and I get the strongest arguments I can. I think Don Marquis has a good secular pro-life argument, and some of my very good students picked up on that. . . . So [some students] in the end were giving a pro-life argument and it was very interesting and got a little heated. So that's what I do: I make the best arguments that I can, and I actually enjoy it. It's a challenge for me.[9]

McAvoy and Hess found that students who participated in well-planned, controversial political discussions benefitted in multiple ways. One big benefit was that discussions allowed students to realize, often for the first time, that their peers disagreed with them, a key part of being a citizen in a democracy. The researchers worry that the twenty-first-century polarized climate creates many more like-minded schools in which teachers and students see the world more or less the same way—a big problem for democracy.

For like-minded schools, encouraging discussions about opposing points of view becomes even more important. Students who practiced discussion also became more interested in politics in a social way, and shared political thoughts with family, friends, and coworkers. And perhaps most importantly, students who participated in Best Practice discussions were more likely to display the kind of interest in political activities—from reading the news to listening to people with different views to being more interested in politics in general—that predict future civic and political engagement.

McAvoy and Hess argue strongly for more classes serving a wider range of students to engage in the kind of deliberations that prepare young people for participating in democracy. "Democratic education requires teachers to create a political classroom in which young people develop the skills, knowledge, and dispositions that allow them to collectively make decisions about how we ought to live together," they wrote.[10]

DEBATE TEAM FOR THE TWENTY-FIRST CENTURY

In his first years as debate coach, high school English teacher Scott Wunn approached debate team in the same way he did when he coached wrestling: both wrestling and debate were competitions that required intense focus and fierce collective energy in order to win. They appeared to be individual competitions, but couldn't be further from the truth—both fed off the energy and experience of the whole group. Both required resistance training and development of core skills to succeed. And in order to win a debate or a wrestling match, the opponent must not be ignored or circumvented, but overcome.

But in the 10 years he coached debate at a high school in Des Moines, Iowa, Wunn found the more he immersed himself in the team, the more he learned. Unlike wrestling matches, each academic debate was unique and brought new challenges—how to make a point, a counterpoint, how to support an argument—and Wunn found himself a more well-rounded thinker. His teaching practice improved, and so did his research skills.

Helping students prepare to argue both sides of an assigned topic nuanced his worldview, providing Wunn with what he calls "a stronger understanding of the gray area of life." Debate and wrestling weren't as alike as he first thought, and he figured that the skills he was gaining must also be happening with his students. Over the years, a more complex view took shape regarding the skills that debate provided for kids, bigger than simply winning or losing a well-planned argument. Wunn noticed that debaters picked up crucial skills that colleges and businesses alike said they were looking for in young people, like the ability to collaborate with team members and think critically about a topic—often this happened not in the library but on their feet, responding to an opponent during a debate. The twenty-first-century skills making headlines were developed naturally during the process of researching, preparing, and participating in a debate.

In addition, the new millennium brought digital technology to debate topics and gave debaters greater access to information than ever before. Access to the internet made student arguments more nuanced and more complex, the depth of analysis more robust. Information gave students power; debates at the turn of the new century, Wunn said, became much more *real*, and students found the immediacy of bringing current events scraped off the web into their debates intoxicating.

All of these collective factors put together have ignited a large debate revival, one that's remodeled itself for the new century. Wunn became executive director of the National Speech and Debate Association in 2003, and began working to transform the association, adding 60,000 students nationwide to the association's membership as well as adding a popular new category of debate that focuses on issues surrounding current events.

Under Wunn's direction, an after-school club with a reputation for incubating future Alex P. Keatons—argumentative young men in nubucks and ties, interested in the intricacies of international policy—has opened its once-closed circle to increasing numbers of young women and people of color. The association hosts an annual national tournament with more than 3,000 students participating, and now sponsors a global debate team of 12 high schoolers that travel the world. They've qualified for the World Schools Debating Championship, what Wunn called the "Olympics" of debate.

Though Wunn has been working toward debate domination for more than 15 years, he said the biggest surge of interest has come in the last four or five as polarization has increased and political rhetoric in the public eye has gotten more heated. In debate, Wunn noted, debaters must be prepared to argue both sides of an issue in order to win, which he said gives them a piece currently missing from political conversations they might encounter on social media.

More educators have reached out to the group because they're concerned about civic engagement skills and civil discourse, as well as teaching students the importance of face-to-face communication. It didn't hurt that Parkland activist David Hogg kept referring to himself as a "debate nerd," either. Every middle and high school in Broward County, Florida, where Parkland is located, has a debate program, and debate instruction begins in fourth grade.[11] With a new category called Public Forum, Wunn has worked to make debate more classroom-friendly. Teachers can have two teams of two students debate a current event topic such as immigration or health care for 40 minutes and still have time left over for reflection and discussion.

Some have suggested that debate not be relegated to social studies class or an after-school club, but be integrated into every subject. Economist Robert Litan has argued for a "counterintuitive" solution to nationwide polarization and cable TV shouting matches: "debatify" more subjects, and allow students to treat other subjects—science, literature—with the same rigorous research and argumentation practices given to world politics and policies. Litan argues that debate isn't only fun, but also provides a kind of resilience training for hearing other points of view.[12]

Expanding debate's reach isn't easy, as it still remains largely an activity for whiter, wealthier kids. But recent research has shown the promise of debate in urban minority communities; in one 2011 study of the Chicago Urban Debate League, debaters were more likely "to graduate from high school, performed better on the ACT, and showed greater gains in cumulative GPA relative to similar comparison students," even after researchers controlled for self-selection into the activity.[13]

But Wunn wants to make debate even more inclusive. In Wunn's perfect world, all young people, no matter their background, would be equipped with the skills debate provides—civil discourse and the ability to see and understand key arguments about both sides of pressing issues. Debaters don't flinch when information is thrown at them, he said. They know how to use information, how to substantiate their arguments, how to understand the legitimate positions of all sides. To be citizens of the twenty-first century, to have the focus to overcome opponents, to win. Like the verbal version of wrestling—except with more informed citizens and a more equitable democracy as the prize at the end of a match.

FOR TEACHERS TO THINK ABOUT

- Civil discourse and debate are important parts of the new civics, and deliberation of controversial issues is one of the six proven practices outlined in the *Guardian of Democracy* report. Practice in civil discourse and discussion of controversial topics incorporate the twenty-first-century seven survival skills, such as communication, accessing and analyzing information, and curiosity.
- Because of community sorting, polarization, and the uncivil nature of current politics, students often come to school having had few or no opportunities to hear opinions or beliefs that differ from their own, or from their families.
- Classroom discussions that lead to meaningful learning require lots of advance planning and guidance from a teacher, but during discussions of controversial topics, students should talk to each other, not to the teacher.

FOR PARENTS TO THINK ABOUT

- Do you live in a cultural or political bubble? Do your kids have the opportunity to hear political opinions or beliefs that differ from what you believe at home? Consider where there may be opportunities to introduce kids to opposing viewpoints, when watching the news or around the dinner table.
- Take opportunities to play "devil's advocate" with your kids to give them a chance to consider another point of view: when complaining about an incident at school or a current event, ask them to consider the other side—how do they think a friend or teacher sees what happened?

Chapter Thirteen

The Future's Citizen

Can Action Civics Create a More Equitable Democracy?

The revolution will not be tweeted.

—Malcolm Gladwell

Edwin O.[1] slid into a chair on the first day of Mr. Rhodes's government class, not thinking much would come of it—he was just one semester away from graduating and being done. He'd heard that the class, which he needed to pass to graduate, would teach kids like him how to have "a voice in the community," but he wasn't sure exactly what that meant and was deeply skeptical. He'd never say it out loud, but he found the whole idea of putting his voice "out there" in Oklahoma City, where he and the majority of his friends and classmates attended U.S. Grant High School on the southwest side of town, laughable. They were just teenagers and nearly all Hispanic, and many of them had parents, grandparents, sisters, and brothers who were undocumented. *Nobody really wants us here, who is going to care what we have to say? What would we even say? This is something I have to do pass. Let's just get this over with.*

Then Mr. Rhodes walked in with a relaxed manner and easy laugh. He began class with an honest conversation, one that Edwin said he didn't "sugarcoat": this wasn't going to be a normal high school government class, with worksheets and tests. Instead of teaching *about* civics, in this class they were going to *do* civics.

Another way of saying "doing civics" was *action civics*, Rhodes told the students, and it was going to be an opportunity for students to reach out to people in their local government and to people in the community, and let them know what was really going on with them. He knew some students in the class were unsure that anybody wanted to hear what they had to say, and he understood—he also came from what he called "the struggle." He told them as a black man in America, they shared some of the same struggles; he also knew what it was like to feel like no one cared what you thought about the place where you lived or went to school. But if students would trust him, he was going to show them that the action civics class might lead them to better understand the system that put them in this position, a cycle of poverty and unequal opportunities in life, and then maybe they would get out of high school and become the policy makers to change things in their communities.

Rhodes told the students about a Black Lives Matter march he and his wife attended, about the threats they received, but how ultimately the police protected them through the march and it turned out a peaceful event. The prospect of speaking out could be scary, but that shouldn't stop them from trying. "If you don't work to change your community, nobody else will. You either choose to continue in the struggle, or choose to overcome it," he said. "You either let the world change who you are, or let who you are change the world."

Edwin wanted to hear more. Mr. Rhodes was the first person he'd en-countered in school to be honest with students about who they were and their place in society. Mr. Rhodes talked to them about how the American dream looked different for people like them, about the fear their communities faced every day. Rhodes told the students that it doesn't have to be that way, that all the people whom the system treats unfairly—including the white rural folks who faced many of the same hurdles as their community did in down-town Oklahoma City—should come together and try and make change in-stead of being divided.

Rhodes told the students it makes America better when we talk about the struggles that minorities have—it is a part of America. Questioning the government isn't unpatriotic, Rhodes told them; it's the most patriotic thing to do, because then we can make America better. Then we can really make liberty and justice for all. Rhodes asked the students to give action civics a chance. Along with the other students, Edwin—still skeptical—said he would try and that he wanted to get involved.

"Now," Mr. Rhodes said. "What are the issues facing your community? Let's make a list."

UNDERSTANDING THE STRUGGLE

Drew Rhodes grew up both in South Oklahoma City and in the suburbs in Midwest City, Oklahoma, near Tinker Air Force base, and comes from a long line of educators. His family has been in the teaching profession since the time of slavery. His mother, maternal grandparents, uncle, and cousin were all teachers, and he grew up hearing stories of his great-greats teaching black children to read in secret, in the far southern parts of Louisiana when literacy was illegal for slaves.

His maternal grandmother grew up in Jim Crow–era Arkansas, where she was witness to unspeakable atrocities; his grandfather was active in Oklahoma City during the civil rights movement of the late 1950s and 1960s. Rhodes's grandfather was part of a group of activists performing sit-ins at coffee shops and restaurants throughout Oklahoma City, and then spread into the rural areas until they were fully integrated. In Sapulpa, Oklahoma, his grandfather had a gun pulled on him for trying to order a sandwich at a "whites only" lunch counter. Rhodes grew up well versed in his own history and the history of black American struggle, and told himself that when he became a teacher, he'd tell his students about it.

He got his degree and began teaching at U.S. Grant High School in 2009, where he taught ninth-grade Oklahoma History and another class called Human Geography, where Rhodes said he got a chance to tell the kids—75 percent of whom were Hispanic and 100 percent qualified for free and reduced lunch—about the *why of where*. The study of human geography is about why conflict happens in certain places, and how places in conflict often share the same characteristics—poor education, poor infrastructure, and corrupt government.

He often asked kids to see how some of the far-flung places they studied—North Korea, the Gaza strip—had similarities to what he called the "American ghettos" of Detroit and East St. Louis, wanting students to understand the systems in place that created cycles of oppression and poverty. He taught classes year after year, always on the lookout for ways to make a connection for his students about how history and government weren't just in books but relevant to who they were and where they lived right now.

Then in 2017 he got a call from Amy Curran, who was opening an Oklahoma City branch of a New York City nonprofit called Generation Citizen. Over the last few years, Generation Citizen had implemented a new kind of civics curriculum called action civics into low-income, mostly minority schools in New York City and Boston, and was getting positive feedback—the gist of it being that students would no longer only learn about the workings of government in the abstract, but instead learn about the government by being active participants in the process of government redress. They'd do it through projects they themselves selected about an issue currently ongoing in their community, preferably one that affected them or their families directly. Curran wanted to know if Rhodes would be interested in teaching one of these classes. Without hesitation, Rhodes called her back and said he was interested. Though human geography had been interesting, action civics was exactly the road he'd been looking for.

ACTION CIVICS: AN OASIS IN A CIVIC DESERT

On the other side of town, Amy Curran had been busy trying to save her kids' elementary school. After years as an executive in the nonprofit world, she had taken a 10-year break to raise her kids in midtown Oklahoma City and ended up being an advocate for the public arts integration school she saw making a difference in her kids' lives, but in the spring of 2016 there had been a huge, statewide funding cut. The cut had been the final straw in a years-long string of funding cuts, and Curran watched as it turned the whole district into the education version of *The Hunger Games*, with schools fighting for their very existence.

She began attending school board meetings and researching school funding to try to figure out what happened, and uncovered lots of other issues the district had been facing for decades, including a dysfunctional school board and a half-hearted attempt at racial integration that had stalled. School board meetings got heated, there was screaming and villainizing people from the part of town you weren't from, and at the end of it all, there were the budget cuts that threatened the day-to-day existence of the already struggling schools.

At the moment of despair that spring and at the behest of a friend, Curran attended a meeting in Oklahoma City with Scott Warren, Generation Citizen's cofounder who was looking to bring the classes to Oklahoma. Warren, the son of a U.S. State Department employee who had lived all over the world, had started the program in his dorm room at Brown in 2008 with dreams of activism and making a difference.

Living in Kenya, Zimbabwe, and throughout Latin America as a kid, Warren had watched governments in developing countries attempt democracy that both succeeded and failed, and he recognized the power and the fragility of democracy and wanted to be an agent of change. He'd seen how crucial democracy was to young people in developing countries, how relevant it was to their lives, and wanted to bring that to the United States, to underrepresented American communities. People who "had been told their entire lives that their voices don't matter," Warren said. "When you walk into school and it's got dilapidated walls, the message the government is sending you is that your voice doesn't matter, at least it doesn't matter as much as others."

Around the same time, other idealistic young Americans had the same idea, and Warren began to brainstorm with people like Bryan Whalen, of Chicago's Mikva Challenge.[2] Together they came to the conclusion that in order to make a more equitable democracy, they'd have to teach people, starting at a young age, not just that they could make a difference, but how. And if introduced in schools, action civics—a term that Warren wasn't exactly sure where it originated, but perfectly described what he was aiming to do—was the way to do it. Generation Citizen was born out of that idea.

As Warren told his story and the story of Generation Citizen in Oklahoma City that night, Curran had a sort of "a-ha" moment. Maybe action civics was what she had been looking for to help her struggling, suicidal school district: a way to teach people how to get involved in government and solve issues. "The reason we are in this mess [school funding crisis], the reason people don't understand how school funding works, is because they didn't get civics education," Curran said. "If you're a professional in the community, you feel like you should know how it all works. And unless you have the time to ask a lot of questions, you go on assumptions that are not necessarily accurate. And if you're not educated, you think that if someone has a college degree, they should automatically know what they're doing. So few people in Oklahoma have anything past a high school diploma, you think it's the right thing to do to pass the buck to someone you think is educated. Then it's easy for those people to manipulate the system if they want to, because people don't know themselves the right questions to ask."

Changing the dynamic required that the details of how democracy worked be taught in school. Like many states, Oklahoma had abandoned civics education decades ago, and also (or as a result) had one of the lowest voting rates in the nation. After hearing Warren talk, Curran signed on to run a Generation Citizen office in Oklahoma City, and in the fall of 2016—in the middle of the divisive 2016 presidential election—she started recruiting schools to use their curriculum, especially those in disconnected areas with low civic participation like Oklahoma's outlying rural areas and Oklahoma City's urban center.

Schools expressed enthusiasm to try action civics, but Curran ran into multiple roadblocks actually getting it into schools—the rural districts were more skeptical, and Curran found she needed to step back and build relationships. Recent research has shown that many rural areas have few opportunities to participate in civic life and are essentially "civic deserts," a concept also discussed in chapter 8.[3] Like urban "food deserts" without a nearby grocery store to provide fresh food, civic deserts are increasingly common in rural and urban districts where twentieth-century civic institutions—in particular churches and religious congregations, unions, local newspapers, and grassroots local politics—are in decline or have disappeared.

In a 2016 study, the Center for Information and Research on Civic Learning and Engagement (CIRCLE) at Tufts University found that nearly 60 percent of rural residents and 30 percent of urban and suburban residents lived in civic deserts, areas "devoid of opportunities for civic and political engagement, such as youth programming, culture and arts organizations, and religious organizations."[4] Not surprisingly, areas with few opportunities to experience civic engagement show poor indicators of civic health and may contribute to alienation. Researcher Kei Kawashima-Ginsberg referred to sociologist Arlie Russell Hochschild's book *Strangers in Their Own Land* when she wrote, "Residents of a community experiencing a severe lack of access to government resources, opportunities for advancement and a decline in community cohesion may develop a sense of alienation from and distrust in aspects of civic life, such as community organizations, government agencies—and even neighbors."[5] In civic deserts, citizens vote and volunteer less often and are less likely to participate in more informal ways, like helping a neighbor.

Once the rural districts were sold on trying action civics, practical concerns got in the way. In the rural community of Pawhuska, an isolated and poor majority Native American area three hours from Oklahoma City, action civics had to be delayed at the beginning of the school year because of water main breaks that shut down the whole district for two weeks. Then once school resumed, the middle and high school principal was out for weeks with a sick family member. The schools had problems aligning the curriculum, too—Pawhuska only had a county government, which wasn't accounted for in the action civics curriculum.

A high school in nearby Enid was excited to start action civics, but when the principal's family member passed away and then the government teacher left, action civics lost an entire school year. And there were hangups in the city, too: a low-income high school in Oklahoma City that had implemented action civics found out two days before Civics Day, in which students present their semester-long projects to local civic leaders and legislators, that they were short a bus driver and might not be able to make it to the statehouse downtown (they ended up securing a bus at the last minute). There were also successes, especially in schools closer to Curran in urban Oklahoma City and the suburbs. Yet even with the successes, Curran found it hard not to get discouraged, as there seemed to be so many mountains to climb.

"We talk a lot about the civics education gap, stemming a lot from the socioeconomic status of a lot of our students, but we also have another gap happening in Oklahoma, and I made up my own term: 'geographic civic engagement gap,'" she said, referring to Oklahoma's spot on the American map. "We feel so far removed from things happening on the coasts, which is where things seem to be happening, we are disengaging even more locally. We should be engaging more locally, but it seems like people back away even further. Few people that I have talked to feel represented by our nationally elected folks. And a ton of Oklahomans have never left the state. When you put all that together, it makes sense why we are so disengaged."

TEENS LEARN HOW TO TAKE ACTION

Generation Citizen's goal is to expand what a civics or government class entails to make it more relevant to students. When he started, Warren's mission was to take the traditional notion of a civics class—in which a teacher explains *how* the government works—and use it as a springboard to let students become part of it, with the idea that if students could see how laws and community decisions get made, they would no longer think that their voices didn't matter. The curriculum doesn't just revolve around a plan of action, but is both academically rigorous and aligned to state standards, and relies heavily on students researching and understanding policies as much as the "taking action" part. Lessons include multiple ways to engage with government such as how to develop an argument, how to gather support from the community and legislators, and how to form a core group of support to lobby, write an editorial for the paper, or organize a protest. Generation Citizen partners with teachers, providing support and coaching throughout the project as well as connections to content experts and civic leaders to help learn details about policy.

The action civics class Edwin was in at U.S. Grant was one of the first to participate with Generation Citizen Oklahoma, and after some debate and guidance from Mr. Rhodes, the class decided they wanted to work on immigration issues (Rhodes said immigration was a popular topic in all his classes, since many of the kids or their families were recent immigrants). Edwin's class researched and wrote a bill that would allow undocumented workers to obtain Oklahoma driver's licenses. Under current Oklahoma law, applying for a driver's license required two pieces of ID, one being a Social Security card unattainable for the undocumented. The class was split into different groups and tasked with different aspects of the project. Edwin's group was in charge of taking the pulse of local businesses and other community members, asking whether they supported the bill. When they reached out, mostly by phone, they got a lot of reactions. Some said they supported the bill, while others took the opportunity to tell the teens that they didn't care what happened to immigrants; some even said they believed they shouldn't even be in this country.

Even though he knew the negative responses reflected the current position of the Trump White House, Edwin was upset and frustrated. His parents had come to the United States undocumented from Mexico nearly 30 years before, living for 25 of those in Las Vegas, Nevada, where Edwin and his younger brother and sister were born. His father worked as a plumber and his mother as a food worker in a hotel, until his father found it harder and harder to keep steady work. They had family in Oklahoma City, and five years ago decided to pick up their family and move there.

It wasn't until they arrived that his parents realized they wouldn't be able to switch their legal Nevada licenses to Oklahoma. Every four years, Edwin's parents have had to go back to Nevada to renew their licenses. Edwin wanted to get the bill passed to make their lives easier, "so they don't have to worry so much." But he also wanted to make the lives of all undocumented workers living in Oklahoma—an estimated 95,000—easier, too.

Rhodes encouraged the class reach out to state representative Mickey Dollens, who had been working on an actual driver's license bill at the statehouse, to share their ideas. In the class version of the bill, students focused on reducing the number of identification forms needed from two to one, making it easier for undocumented immigrants to obtain a license. Also included in the class bill was changing the $5 license to $25, with the difference flowing to the public schools.

After spending three months of class time on the project, on a sunny day in May a handful of chosen delegates from Rhodes's class headed down to the Oklahoma State Capitol building for Civics Day. Throughout the day, delegates from action civics classes all over the city presented their projects in front of nearly 60 local politicians, business owners, and other civic leaders, who awarded prizes in different categories to the best projects like the "Grassroots Change" award for the project with the most local roots, and the "Diversity" award, which focused on how many different perspectives students obtained for their chosen issue.

But on the morning of the big event, Mr. Rhodes wasn't sure his classes were going to make it—they'd lost two whole weeks of class time due to the statewide teacher walkouts, and all the time out of school had students behind on their presentations. Just a few hours before they were due to present, students were still huddled in groups in class, frantically pasting information on poster boards and practicing their speeches in whispers.

Though time was a factor, what Rhodes worried about most was that the student disorganization also reflected their state of mind about the work they'd been doing all semester—being active participants in their local government. Rhodes had never taught a class quite like action civics, and though he didn't show it, he was unsure how it would turn out. Students had started the class skeptical, and Rhodes thought they might still be questioning whether their work would be taken seriously. But Edwin's group presentation went off without a hitch, and at the end of Civics Day, Mr. Rhodes received the "Teacher Changemaker" award.

The class was buoyed by the response of the local community on Civics Day; Rhodes felt that his classes had really made an impact. "Action civics is when you get to reach out to the legislators, the researchers, and hit them with this powerful struggle that they can't deny," Rhodes said. "They listen to your experience as a human being, and [at Civics Day] we saw that transformation the legislators had. Once you have that interaction, they can't go back to being the same legislator they were. Action civics does not have a color, it fits to the mold of what that community needs. For me as an educator—I'm an old-school educator, when you come into my house, which is what I call my classroom, I love you and you're my family. I'm going to plant a seed of inspiration. I spend every day trying to give that inspiration to my kids. That's where we have to be at as a country, we need to teach with love, compassion, understanding. That's the American Dream."

IS ACTION CIVICS WHAT WE NEED RIGHT NOW?

Defending democratic values in the twenty-first century may more than simply benefit from action civics; it may well require it. As the nation becomes more polarized, trust in government and other civic institutions tanks, and traditional liberal democracy ("liberal" in this case meaning the classical republic of the founders, not left-wing) becomes more at risk, raising a young army of uncomplacent, action-oriented citizens willing to do the hard work of participation appears to some as a promising solution.

Proponents of action civics imagine that students who learn that they can be agents of change will then grow up to volunteer in political parties, head community committees, and form associations—three critical places where American civic participation has fallen off the map. But those proponents would also be happy if students left high school simply having a better understanding of how the government works, and how their participation can make a difference in outcomes.

Action civics' emphasis on students knowing and understanding what it takes to change communities from the inside was designed to build the civic knowledge, skills, and dispositions young people need in order to participate in a twenty-first-century democracy that is hands-off for the vast majority of Americans. The idea is to get students to look around at the political, social, and cultural problems within their community and guide them to finding solutions, and then students would not only get a taste of the theory of democracy, but get their hands dirty in the slow, deliberative process of making change.

Though the vast majority of today's students don't get action civics in class—at least not yet—the movement is growing and gaining popularity. At the time of this writing, the two largest action civics organizations together have educated nearly 34,000 students: Generation Citizen's program has reached about 18,000 students in six states; the Mikva Challenge, in Chicago, Washington, DC, and California, has reached about 16,000. Nearly 20 smaller organizations are also offering action civics for schools.

In addition, several states are looking at adding an action civics portion to already existing curricula. In Florida, one of the only states to require students to pass a civics course, advocates at the nonprofit Joint Center for Citizenship are considering ways to add action civics–like "informed action" projects to their already robust civics curriculum. And new legislation for beefing up civics education in Massachusetts has hands-on action civics projects built into the new standards.

But Massachusetts governor Charlie Baker pushed back on the action civics requirement, suggesting that action civics projects could easily be partisan—a class project focused on gun control or expanding gun rights, for example, could easily slip into political ideology—and wanted to ensure that students wouldn't be forced to participate in a project that didn't align with their personal convictions.

Baker sent back the civics bill, which had already passed the Massachusetts legislature, with an amendment requiring schools to make action civics projects non-partisan and to allow alternative opportunities for students who didn't want to participate. In the amendment letter, Baker worried that projects might narrow the ideas on policy solutions to community problems to which students are exposed. He wrote that "an informed citizenry, fully exposed to a wide variety of ideas, is critical to our democracy . . . we must be thoughtful as to how we approach the instruction of civics, always ensuring in our classrooms that differing points of view are afforded impartial consideration."[6]

Other action civics critics are more concerned about the message students come away with long after projects are finished. In his essay "Civics Education Should Focus on Critical Thinking, Not Activism," former Harvard history professor and Massachusetts candidate for U.S. Senate John Muresianu worried that action civics classes focus too much on taking action and not enough on the difficult and often complex deliberating that leads to deciding, *what should we do about this community problem?* It's easy to say, "something should be done"; much harder is deciding what that something is. "'Getting out the vote' and engaging in activism should only come after students have weighed the arguments on every side of each issue," Muresianu wrote;[7] he believes that critical thinking, one of the core twenty-first-century skills mentioned at the start of this book, should be the main focus of civics class.

To illustrate, he used the example issue of whether or not the government should raise the minimum wage to $15. Muresianu said students should be taught like this: first, introduce students to the multiple ideas on raising the minimum wage, from Bernie Sanders's stance to those of pro-market traditionalists. Then students need to learn the facts—the research on whether or not a higher minimum wage would help bring people out of poverty is mixed; some reliable studies conclude a higher minimum wage would raise unemployment, while others find no change. Students should be shown how to come to a decision when facts conflict, how to "evaluate studies and reports in order to figure out which papers present better data."[8]

Muresianu admitted in the essay that approaching civics this way is a long and complicated way to teach, and strongly advocated for civics education to start much earlier. "Learning civics, like learning a second language, requires constant thinking, speaking and writing," he wrote. "In order to train the next generation of citizens and voters, we need a serious approach to civics education that focuses on critical thinking before action."[9]

THE FUTURE'S MORE ACTIVE CITIZEN

Action civics hasn't been around long enough to study what kind of long-term effects it might have on young adults' future civic engagement, but some short-term surveys show promise. Chicago-based Mikva Challenge reports that graduates from their action civics program have much higher rates of voter registration among young people (88 percent) compared to non-participants (53 percent), and higher rates of volunteering.[10]

In their 2018 impact report, Generation Citizen found that teachers reported that 76 percent of their students increased their civic knowledge through the program, and anecdotally teachers reported that they believed the largest share of civic knowledge acquisition involved "local political structures and processes,"[11] which is exactly what Scott Warren hoped for—that students would learn, as the saying goes, that all politics is local. He said in the short term, Generation Citizen students are voting at higher rates, but they'll need to wait and see whether these effects last over time.

Edwin, who graduated from U.S. Grant in May 2018, is now attending Oklahoma City Community College in the mornings and working on plumbing jobs with his dad in the afternoons. He has plans to transfer to a larger university in a couple of years, to earn a degree in criminal justice. He was unsure of what happened with the driver's license bill he worked on in class last year, but has remained close with Mr. Rhodes. Edwin talked with him over lunch about his plans to become a police officer and change the institution from the inside out, how he wants to help officers and the public become more trusting of each other. He credits Mr. Rhodes's class with helping him think about public life in a different way, as something he should want to be a part of.

It's this idea—thinking of public life as the citizen's domain, not the exclusive rights of "others"—that Warren is chipping away at, day by day. Some of Generation Citizen's state operations, like the one in Massachusetts, have been offering this idea not just to classrooms but statehouses as well, advocating to change civics education policy at the state level—a move that Warren said is both necessary and insufficient.

Warren dreams of civics working its way to the public both from the top down (state policy) and the bottom up (Mr. Rhodes), and getting educators and school districts and lawmakers to think of civics in a new way, not as a class tacked on to a lifetime of education in the spring of senior year—*one more thing before you go, learn how our country works, and your place in it*—but comprehensively educating for democracy, beginning the day kindergarten students walk into school. In many ways, Warren wants the same things Seth Andrew does at Democracy Prep, working democratic questions into every class—a science class that asks, how clean is the water that we drink? How clean is the air that we breathe? How can we change that? Or a math class with problems to help students better understand crucial questions about our communities, from how much money is in the budget to how we should pay public employees. In short, an entire education system that asks its students democracy's essential question: "How should we live together?"[12]

Scott Warren is an action civics true believer. He said that despite criticisms, he still thinks action civics is a way to get to the root of democracy's challenges and create the next generation of citizens—to allow students to grapple with the complexity of policy, and show them they have the power to make things better. "It's different from traditional civics, which, to generalize, often says 'let's learn how great American government is,' or 'the system is too irrevocably broken to do anything about it,'" he said. "The first one is disempowering; the second one is false."

"American history is about working toward including more people, and in many ways we have succeeded. Any time there has been positive change in this country, young people have been at the forefront. And at this moment in time, when people are distrustful about the future, there is a necessity in working with young people to create the democracy, the idealism that we need," he said. "I think it's a necessity."

FOR TEACHERS TO THINK ABOUT

- Action civics is a key component of the new civics, and was recently added as a "practice to watch" among the *Guardian of Democracy* report's proven practices, as research is beginning to accumulate showing its effectiveness in increasing civic knowledge and skills. Hands-on action civics projects incorporate several of the seven survival skills for the twenty-first century, including collaboration, critical thinking, and accessing and analyzing information.
- For action civics projects to be effective learning tools, they need a strong base of information about government agencies, levers of power, and how

government works, as well as an engaging project idea. They also need to consider the belief systems of all the students in the class.

- Though limited research is available, civics proponents believe action civics is one of the most effective ways to show young people how local government functions and how everyday citizens can create community change, and is especially effective for students who may be disenfranchised from their communities or feel their voices don't matter.

FOR PARENTS TO THINK ABOUT

- Action civics projects aimed at making community change are not limited to classrooms, but could also be implemented in scouts, religious youth groups, community centers, student councils, and after-school clubs.
- Action civics projects aren't limited to high school students, but could be adapted for middle schoolers, too.
- It's never too early for kids to see democracy in action and learn how to make positive change in their communities. Make getting involved in your community a family affair: if neighbors get together to lobby the city for a sidewalk or a new library, take your child along to the meetings and give them the opportunity to see how citizens interact with local government.

Notes

INTRODUCTION

1. Thomas Jefferson, in a letter to Edward Everett, 1824, ME 16:22, https://founders.archives.gov/documents/Jefferson/98-01-02-4143; and Jefferson, in a letter to Henry Dearborn, 1822, FE 10:237, https://founders.archives.gov/documents/Jefferson/98-01-02-3131.

2. Robert Pondiscio and Kate Stringer, "On Constitution Day, In Search of the Public Mission of Schools," Thomas B. Fordham Institute, September 26, 2015, https://fordhaminstitute.org/national/commentary/constitution-day-search-public-mission-schools.

3. For NAEP U.S. history scores, see https://nces.ed.gov/nationsreportcard/ushistory/; for NAEP civics scores, see https://nces.ed.gov/nationsreportcard/civics/.

4. "Americans Are Poorly Informed about Constitutional Provisions," Annenberg Public Policy Center, September 12, 2017, https://www.annenbergpublicpolicycenter.org/americans-are-poorly-informed-about-basic-constitutional-provisions/.

5. David E. Campbell, Meira Levinson, and Frederick M. Hess, *Making Civics Count: Citizen Education for a New Generation* (Cambridge, MA: Harvard Education Press, 2012), 2.

6. Drew Silver, "U.S. Trails Most Developed Countries in Voter Turnout," Pew Research Center, May 21, 2018, http://www.pewresearch.org/fact-tank/2018/05/21/u-s-voter-turnout-trails-most-developed-countries/.

7. "Public Trust in Government 1958–2017," Pew Research Center, December 14, 2017, http://www.people-press.org/2017/12/14/public-trust-in-government-1958-2017/.

8. "Congressional Job Approval," Gallup Poll: Congress and the Public, December 2018, https://news.gallup.com/poll/1600/congress-public.aspx.

9. Jeff Greenfield, "How Political Opponents Became Enemies in the U.S.," PBS Newshour, April 1, 2018, https://www.pbs.org/video/how-political-opponents-became-enemies-in-the-u-s-1522600678/.

10. Roberto Stefan Foa and Yashca Mounk, "The Danger of Deconsolidation," *Journal of Democracy* 27, no. 3 (July 2016): 5.

11. Ibid., 7–14.

12. Francis Fukuyama, *The End of History and the Last Man* (New York: Free Press, 1992).

13. Kei Kawashima-Ginsberg, "The Other 2018 Midterm Wave: A Historic 10-Point Jump in Turnout among Young People," The Conversation, November 8, 2018, https://theconversation.com/the-other-2018-midterm-wave-a-historic-10-point-jump-in-turnout-among-young-people-106505.

1. THE RISE OF THE TWENTY-FIRST-CENTURY CITIZEN

1. Eric Liu, *You're More Powerful Than You Think: A Citizen's Guide to Making Change Happen* (New York: PublicAffairs, 2017), 34.

2. Although no one is sure who coined the term "Generation Z," it is generally used for young people born between 1995 and the early 2000s. Other names for the generation that came after the millennials include iGen, digital natives, and the "plurals."

3. The Immigration and Nationality Act of 1965 for the first time gave equal footing to immigrants from Southern European and non-European countries. See https://cis.org/Report/HartCeller-Immigration-Act-1965.

4. "Nearly Half of Post-Millennials Are Racial or Ethnic Minorities," Pew Research Center, November 13, 2018, http://www.pewsocialtrends.org/2018/11/15/early-benchmarks-show-post-millennials-on-track-to-be-most-diverse-best-educated-generation-yet/psdt-11-15-18_postmillennials-00-00/.

5. "The First Generation of the Twenty-First Century: An Introduction to the Pluralist Generation," Magid Generational Strategies, 2014, https://web.archive.org/web/20160304080730/http://magid.com/sites/default/files/pdf/MagidPluralistGenerationWhitepaper.pdf.

6. Monica Anderson and Jingjing Jiang, "Teens, Social Media and Technology 2018," Pew Research Center, May 31, 2018, http://www.pewinternet.org/2018/05/31/teens-social-media-technology-2018/.

7. "The First Generation of the Twenty-First Century."

8. Jean Twenge, *iGen: Why Today's Super-Connected Kids Are Growing Up Less Rebellious, More Tolerant, Less Happy—and Completely Unprepared for Adulthood—and What That Means for the Rest of Us* (New York: Atria Books, 2017).

9. Statistics compiled from Twenge, *iGen*; and Jean Twenge, "Have Smartphones Destroyed a Generation?" *Atlantic Monthly*, September 2017, https://www.theatlantic.com/magazine/archive/2017/09/has-the-smartphone-destroyed-a-generation/534198/.

10. Anderson and Jiang, "Teens, Social Media."

11. Amy Orben and Andrew K. Przybylski, "The Association between Adolescent Well-Being and Digital Technology Use," *Nature Human Behaviour* 3 (2019): 173–82.

12. Jonathan Haidt and Greg Lukianoff, *The Coddling of the American Mind: How Good Intentions and Bad Ideas Are Setting Up a Generation for Failure* (New York: Penguin, 2018).

13. Bill Bishop, *The Big Sort: Why the Clustering of Like-Minded America Is Tearing Us Apart* (New York: Houghton Mifflin, 2008).

14. C. West Churchman, "Free for All," *Management Science* 14, no. 4 (December 1967): 141–46.

15. "What's More Important?" Heartland Monitor Poll conducted by Allstate, 2015, http://heartlandmonitor.com/whats-more-important/.

16. "2016 Millennial Impact Report," Achieve Research Agency, 2016, http://www.themillennialimpact.com/past-research.

17. "Second Generation Americans: A Portrait of the Adult Children of Immigrants," Pew Research Center, February 7, 2013, http://www.pewsocialtrends.org/2013/02/07/second-generation-americans/.

18. Tony Wagner, *The Global Achievement Gap: Why Even Our Best Schools Don't Teach the New Survival Skills Our Children Need—and What We Can Do about It* (New York: Basic Books, 2014), xv.

19. Adapted from Wagner, *Global Achievement Gap.*

20. Andrew Guess, Brendan Nyhan, and Jason Reifler, "Selective Exposure to Misinformation: Evidence from the Consumption of Fake News during the 2016 U.S. Presidential Campaign," European Research Council, January 2018.

21. Soroush Vosoughi, Deb Roy, and Sinan Aral, "The Spread of True and False News Online," *Science* 359, no. 6380 (March 2018).

22. Joseph Kahne and Benjamin Bowyer, "Educating for Democracy in a Partisan Age: Confronting the Challenges of Motivated Reasoning and Misinformation," *American Educational Research Journal* 54, no. 1 (2017): 3–34, https://doi.org/10.3102/0002831216679817.

23. Daniel T. Willingham, "How Knowledge Helps," American Federation of Teachers, Spring 2006, https://www.aft.org/periodical/american-educator/spring-2006/how-knowledge-helps.

24. *The Civic Mission of Schools 2003* (Carnegie Corporation of New York and the Center for Information and Research on Civic Learning and Engagement, 2003), 4.

25. Jonathan Gould, Kathleen Hall Jamieson, Peter Levine, Ted McConnell, and David B. Smith, eds., *Guardian of Democracy: The Civic Mission of Schools* (Philadelphia: Leonore Annenberg Institute for Civics of the Annenberg Public Policy Center at the University of Pennsylvania, 2011), https://www.carnegie.org/publications/guardian-of-democracy-the-civic-mission-of-schools/.

26. Michael D. Rich and Jennifer Kavanaugh, *Truth Decay: An Initial Exploration of the Diminishing Role of Facts and Analysis in American Public Life* (Santa Monica, CA: Rand Corporation, 2018), https://www.rand.org/pubs/research_reports/RR2314.html.

27. Naomi N. Duke, Carol L. Skay, Sandra L. Pettingell, and Iris W. Borowski, "From Adolescent Connections to Social Capital: Predictors of Civic Engagement in Young Adulthood," *Journal of Adolescent Health* 44, no. 2 (February 2009): 161–68.

28. Quoted in Perri Klass, "What Really Makes Us Vote? It May Be Our Parents," *New York Times*, November 7, 2016, https://www.nytimes.com/2016/11/07/well/family/what-really-makes-us-vote-it-may-be-our-parents.html.

2. NURSERIES OF A FREE REPUBLIC

1. Thomas Jefferson, "Bill for the More General Diffusion of Knowledge" (1778), The Jefferson Monticello: Quotes and Letters, http://tjrs.monticello.org/letter/58.

2. Dana Goldstein, *The Teacher Wars: A History of America's Most Embattled Profession* (New York: Doubleday, 2014), 29.

3. Renee Critcher Lyons, *Teaching Civics in the Library: An Instructional and Historical Guide for Public and School Librarians* (Jefferson, NC: McFarland & Company, 2015), 13.

4. "The Perpetuation of Our Political Institutions (Address by Abraham Lincoln before the Young Men's Lyceum of Springfield, January 27, 1838)," *Journal of the Abraham Lincoln Association* 6, no. 1 (1984): 6–14, http://hdl.handle.net/2027/spo.2629860.0006.103.

5. Peter Levine, *We Are the Ones We Have Been Waiting For: The Promise of Civic Renewal in America* (New York: Oxford University Press, 2013), 137.

6. "William Holmes McGuffey and His Readers," *Museum Gazette*, National Park Service, January 1993, https://www.nps.gov/jeff/learn/historyculture/upload/mcguffey.pdf.

7. Jennifer Bachner, "From Classroom to the Voting Booth: The Effect of High School Civic Education on Turnout," Scribd, September 12, 2010, https://www.scribd.com/document/122825938/From-Classroom-to-Voting-Booth-The-Eff-ect-of-High-School-Civic-Education-on-Turnout-Jennifer-Bachner.

8. Vucina Zoric, "Fundamentals of John Dewey's Concept of Civic Education," *History of Education and Children's Literature* 10, no. 1 (January 2015): 431–32.

9. *The Boy Scout's Handbook, First Edition* (New York: Doubleday, 1911), n.p.

10. The 4-H Pledge, https://4-h.org/about/what-is-4-h/4-h-pledge/.

11. Robert D. Putnam, *Bowling Alone: The Collapse and Revival of American Community* (New York: Simon and Schuster, 2001); see chapter 4.

12. Alexis de Tocqueville, "On the Use That the Americans Make of Associations in Civil Life," from *Democracy in America*, chapter 5, first published in 1835.

13. Greg Lukianoff and Jonathan Haidt, *The Coddling of the American Mind: How Good Intentions and Bad Ideas Are Setting Up a Generation for Failure* (New York: Penguin, 2018), 130.

14. Sheldon M. Stern and Jeremy A. Stern, *The State of State U.S. History Standards* (Washington, DC: Thomas Fordham Institute, 2011), https://fordhaminstitute.org/national/research/state-state-us-history-standards-2011.

15. Beth Morton and Ben Dalton, "Changes in Instructional Hours in Four Subjects by Public School Teachers of Grades 1 Through 4," *Statistics in Brief*, National Center for Education Statistics, May 2007, https://nces.ed.gov/pubs2007/2007305.pdf.

16. "Two-Thirds of Teachers Say Reading, Math Focus Crowding Out Other Core Academic Subjects," Common Core/Farkas Duffett Research Group, December 2008.

17. "Most States Require History, but Not Civics," *Education Week*, October 23, 2018, https://www.edweek.org/ew/section/multimedia/data-most-states-require-history-but-not.html.

18. Robert Pondiscio and Kate Stringer, "On Constitution Day, in Search of the Public Mission of Schools," Thomas Fordham Institute, September 16, 2015, https://fordhaminstitute.org/national/commentary/constitution-day-search-public-mission-schools.

19. Levine, *We Are the Ones*, 137.

20. Michael Hansen, Elizabeth Mann Levesque, Jon Valant, and Diana Quintero, "The 2018 Brown Center Report on American Education," Brookings Institute, June 27, 2018, chapter 1, https://www.brookings.edu/multi-chapter-report/the-2018-brown-center-report-on-american-education/.

21. Ibid.

22. Meira Levinson, "The Civic Empowerment Gap: Defining the Problem and Locating solutions," in *Handbook of Research on Civic Engagement in Youth*, ed. Lonnie R. Sherrod, Judith Torney-Purta, and Constance A. Flanagan (New York: Wiley and Sons, 2010), 319.

23. Ibid., 331.

24. Ibid, 322.

25. William Galston, "Political Knowledge, Political Engagement and Civic Education," *Annual Review of Political Science* 9, no. 4 (2001): 217–34.

26. Meira Levinson, "Civics Empowerment Gap" (video), Chicago Humanities Festival, January 29, 2016, https://www.youtube.com/watch?v=85i650FmpXA.

27. Jim Hand, "State Legislature Passes Civics Education Bill, Local Educators on Board With Idea," *The Sun Chronicle*, July 25, 2018, https://www.thesunchronicle.com/news/local_news/state-legislature-passes-civics-education-bill-local-educators-on-board/article_fc55d813-f4ce-53a0-b3ca-0a1466f3e7de.html.

28. Jerry Cornfield, "Lawmakers Are Pushing Bills to Expand Civics Education," *The Daily Herald*, February 8, 2017, 2:55 p.m., https://www.heraldnet.com/news/lawmakers-are-pushing-bills-to-expand-civics-education/.

29. Emily Cardinali, "What Your State Is Doing to Beef Up Civics Education," NPR, July 21, 2018, https://www.npr.org/sections/ed/2018/07/21/624267576/what-your-state-is-doing-to-beef-up-civics-education.

30. *The College, Career, and Civic Life (C3) Framework for Social Studies State Standards: Guidance for Enhancing the Rigor of K–12 Civics, Economics, Geography, and History* (Silver Spring, MD: NCSS, 2013).

31. Hansen, Mann Levesque, Valant, and Quintero, "Brown Center Report."

32. Bachner, "From the Classroom to the Voting Booth."

3. NEW CIVICS INNOVATOR

1. Brian Gill, Charles Tilley, Emilyn Whitesell, Mariel Finucane, Liz Potamites, and Sean Corcoran, "The Impact of Democracy Prep Public Schools on Civic Participation," Mathematica Policy Research, April 19, 2018, https://www.mathematica-mpr.com/our-publications-and-findings/publications/the-impact-of-democracy-prep-public-schools-on-civic-participation.

4. A TREE WITHOUT ROOTS

1. Diane Ravitch, "Decline and Fall of Teaching History," *New York Times*, November 17, 1985, https://www.nytimes.com/1985/11/17/magazine/decline-and-fall-of-teaching-history.html.

2. Ibid.

3. NAEP, "U.S. History Assessment 2014," https://nces.ed.gov/nationsreportcard/ushistory/.

4. "Two-Thirds of Teachers Say Reading, Math Focus Crowding Out Other Core Academic Subjects," Common Core/Farkas Duffett Research Group, December 2008.

5. "The Marginalization of Social Studies," Council of Chief State School Officers, 2018, https://ccsso.org/sites/default/files/2018-11/Elementary%20SS%20Brief%2045%20Minute%20Version.pdf.

6. "National Survey Finds Just 1 in 3 Americans Would Pass Citizenship Test," Woodrow Wilson National Fellowship Foundation, October 3, 2018, https://woodrow.org/news/national-survey-finds-just-1-in-3-americans-would-pass-citizenship-test/.

7. "Teaching Hard History: American Slavery," Southern Poverty Law Center, 2018, https://www.splcenter.org/sites/default/files/tt_hard_history_american_slavery.pdf.

8. "Holocaust Knowledge and Awareness Study, Executive Summary," Schoen Consulting, April 2018, https://www.jewishvirtuallibrary.org/jsource/images/holocaustknowledgestudy.pdf.

9. Julie Ray, "A Report Card on Teens' Favorite Subjects," Gallup, 2003, https://news.gallup.com/poll/8248/report-card-teens-favorite-subjects.aspx.

10. Daniel T. Willingham, *Why Don't Students Like School?* (San Francisco: Jossey-Bass, 2009), 25.

11. Thanks to Fordham Fellow Robert Pondiscio for the brilliant phrase, "mental furniture."

12. E. D. Hirsch, Jr., *The Making of Americans: Democracy and Our Schools* (New Haven, CT: Yale University Press, 2010); see chapter 6.

13. Michael X. Delli Carpini and Scott Keeter, *What Americans Know About Politics and Why It Matters* (New Haven, CT: Yale University Press, 1997).

14. Meira Levinson, "The Civic Empowerment Gap: Defining the Problem and Locating Solutions," in *Handbook of Research on Civic Engagement in Youth*, ed. Lonnie Sherrod, Judith Torney-Purta, and Constance A. Flanagan (New York: Wiley and Sons, 2010), 321.

15. "Highlights from Education at a Glance 2009," Organization for Economic Cooperation and Development, 2009, https://www.oecd.org/education/skills-beyond-school/43619343.pdf.

16. Natalie Wexler, *The Knowledge Gap: The Hidden Cause of America's Broken Education System—and How to Fix It* (New York: Avery, 2019).

17. Donna R. Recht and Lauren Leslie, "Effect of Prior Knowledge on Good and Poor Readers' Memory of Text," *Journal of Educational Psychology* 80, no. 1 (1988): 16–20.

18. Daniel T. Willingham, "How Knowledge Helps," *American Educator*, Spring 2006, https://www.aft.org/periodical/american-educator/spring-2006/how-knowledge-helps.

19. Daniel T. Willingham, "Critical Thinking: Why Is It So Hard to Teach?" *American Educator*, Summer 2007, https://www.aft.org/sites/default/files/periodicals/Crit_Thinking.pdf.

20. Kate Shuster, "Teaching Hard History," Southern Poverty Law Center, January 2018, https://www.splcenter.org/20180131/teaching-hard-history.

21. Ibid.

22. James W. Loewen, *Lies My Teacher Told Me: Everything Your American History Textbook Got Wrong* (New York: Simon and Schuster, 2007).

23. "Taking Politics Out of Classrooms: Recommendations for Revising the Texas Social Studies Curriculum Standards," Texas Freedom Network Education Fund, February 2018, http://tfn.org/cms/assets/uploads/2018/02/FINAL_SSTEKS_report_2.2018.pdf.

24. Dana Goldstein, "Is the U.S. a Democracy? A Social Studies Battle Turns on the Nation's Values," *New York Times*, April 7, 2019, https://www.nytimes.com/2019/04/07/us/usa-democracy.html.

25. Stephen Sawchuk, "How History Class Divides Us," *Education Week*, October 23, 2018, https://www.edweek.org/ew/projects/how-history-class-divides-us.html.

26. Loewen, *Lies My Teacher Told Me*, 25.

27. Christine Gross-Loh, "A Better Way to Teach History," *Atlantic*, February 8, 2016, https://www.theatlantic.com/education/archive/2016/02/harvard-history-class/460314/.

28. April White, "David Moss Is Rewriting History," Harvard Business School Alumni: Stories, March 2, 2016, https://www.alumni.hbs.edu/stories/Pages/story-impact.aspx?num=5151.

29. Ibid.

30. "Chapter 5: History among the Social Studies," American Historical Association, https://www.historians.org/about-aha-and-membership/aha-history-and-archives/historical-archives/american-history-in-schools-and-colleges/chapter-5-history-among-the-social-studies.

5. *NEW CIVICS INNOVATOR*

1. Asi Burak and Laura Parker, *Power Play: How Video Games Can Save the World* (New York: St. Martin's Press, 2017).

2. Ibid., 38

3. "Power Play: Trends and Opportunities in Gaming for Good with Asi Burak" (video), Joan B. Kroc Institute for Peace and Justice at the University of San Diego, May 2016, https://www.youtube.com/watch?v=6SWidS0wzcA.

4. "Most Teen Boys and Girls Play Video Games," Pew Research Center: Teens, Social Media and Technology 2018, May 29, 2018, https://www.pewinternet.org/2018/05/31/teens-social-media-technology-2018/pi_2018-05-31_teenstech_0-06/.

5. Mark Walsh, "Life Story Fuels Justice Sotomayor's Passion for Education, Civics," *Education Week*, November 1, 2018, https://www.edweek.org/ew/articles/2018/11/01/life-story-fuels-justice-sotomayors-passion-for.html.

6. THE VALUE OF VIRTUE

1. Statistics from surveys and research conducted by Dr. Donald McCabe, International Center for Academic Integrity homepage, 2017, https://academicintegrity.org/statistics/.

2. Zach Miners, "One Third of Teens Use Cellphones to Cheat in School," *U.S. News and World Report*, June 23, 2009, https://www.usnews.com/education/blogs/on-education/2009/06/23/one-third-of-teens-use-cellphones-to-cheat-in-school.

3. Ibid.

4. Maria Puente, "'SNL' Writer Suspended, Apologizes for Barron Trump Tweet," *USA Today*, January 23, 2017, https://www.usatoday.com/story/life/tv/2017/01/23/snl-writer-suspended-apologizes-barron-trump-tweet/96963720/.

5. Barbara Campbell, "Congressman-Elect, Sorry He Hit Reporter, Promises to Donate to Charity," National Public Radio, June 7, 2017, https://www.npr.org/sections/thetwo-way/2017/06/07/531994527/congressman-elect-sorry-he-hit-reporter-promises-donation-to-charity.

6. "Student Reports of Bullying: Results from the 2015 School Crime Supplement to the National Crime Victimization Survey," National Center for Education Statistics, December 2016, https://nces.ed.gov/pubs2017/2017015.pdf.

7. "2018 Hate Crime Statistics," Federal Bureau of Investigation, https://ucr.fbi.gov/hate-crime/2017.

8. "The Trump Effect: The Impact of the 2016 Presidential Election on Our Nation's Schools," Southern Poverty Law Center, November 2016, https://www.splcenter.org/20161128/trump-effect-impact-2016-presidential-election-our-nations-schools.

9. Mark Keierleber, "New FBI Data: School-Based Hate Crimes Jumped 25 Percent Last Year—for the Second Year in a Row," The 74, November 4, 2018, https://www.the74million.org/new-fbi-data-school-based-hate-crimes-jumped-25-percent-last-year-for-the-second-year-in-a-row/.

10. Sandy Cohen, "Bad Behavior Is Trending Online, Inspiring It in Real Life," *Mercury News*, July 10, 2017, https://www.mercurynews.com/2017/07/10/bad-behavior-is-trending-online-inspiring-it-in-real-life/.

11. Jubilee Centre for Character and Virtues, "A Framework for Character Education in Schools," University of Binghamton, August 2017, https://uobschool.org.uk/wp-content/uploads/2017/08/Framework-for-Character-Education-2017-Jubilee-Centre.pdf.

12. Angela Duckworth, *Grit: The Power of Passion and Perseverance* (New York: Scribner, 2016).

13. Paul Tough, *How Children Succeed: Grit, Curiosity, and the Hidden Power of Character* (New York: Houghton Mifflin Harcourt, 2012).

14. Quoted in Kristin Ozelli, "Should Grit Be Taught and Tested in School?" *Scientific American*, July 1, 2016, https://www.scientificamerican.com/article/should-grit-be-taught-and-tested-in-school/.

15. J. A. Durlak, R. P. Weissberg, A. B. Dymnicki, R. D. Taylor, and K. B. Schellinger, "The Impact of Enhancing Students' Social and Emotional Learning: A Meta-Analysis of School-Based Universal Interventions," *Child Development* 82 (2011): 405–32.

16. Jeffrey Aaron Snyder, "Teaching Kids 'Grit' is All the Rage. Here's What's Wrong With It," *New Republic*, May 6, 2014, https://newrepublic.com/article/117615/problem-grit-kipp-and-character-based-education.

17. Making Caring Common Project, "The Children We Mean To Raise: The Real Messages Parents Are Sending About Values," Harvard Graduate School of Education, July 2014, http://mcc.gse.harvard.edu/files/gse-mcc/files/mcc-research-report.pdf?m=1448057487.

18. Mark Ottoni-Wilhelm, David B. Estell, and Neil H. Perdue, "Role-Modeling and Conversations about Giving in the Socialization of Adolescent Charitable Giving and Volunteering," *Journal of Adolescence* 37 (2014): 53–66.

19. Thomas Lickona, *How to Raise Kind Kids: And Get Respect, Gratitude and a Happier Family in the Bargain* (New York: Penguin Books, 2018), 4.

20. Russell Freedman, *Washington at Valley Forge* (New York: Holiday House, 2008).

21. Tenzin Gyatso, fourteenth Dalai Lama, "We Need an Education of the Heart," *Los Angeles Times*, November 13, 2017, https://www.latimes.com/opinion/op-ed/la-oe-dalai-lama-alt-we-need-an-education-of-the-heart-20171113-story.html.

7. NEW CIVICS INNOVATOR

1. Jack Bradley, "I Spend Half My Days in Accelerated Classes and the Other Half in Special Ed," *Hechinger Report*, November 1, 2016, https://hechingerreport.org/spend-half-days-accelerated-classes-half-special-ed/.

8. TOGETHER WE CAN DO SO MUCH

1. Douglas Nemecek, "Cigna U.S. Loneliness Index," May 2018, https://www.cigna.com/assets/docs/newsroom/loneliness-survey-2018-fact-sheet.pdf.

2. D. Russell, L. A. Peplau, and C. E. Cutrona, "The Revised UCLA Loneliness Scale: Concurrent and Discriminant Validity Evidence," *Journal of Personality and Social Psychology* 39 (1980): 472–80.

3. Nemecek, "Cigna U.S. Loneliness Index," 6.

4. Ceylon Yeginsu, "U.K. Appoints a Minister for Loneliness," *New York Times*, January 7, 2018, https://www.nytimes.com/2018/01/17/world/europe/uk-britain-loneliness.html.

5. Robert D. Putnam, *Bowling Alone: The Collapse and Revival of American Community* (New York: Simon and Schuster, 2000).

6. Ibid., 19.

7. Lindsay H. Shaw and Larry M. Grant, "In Defense of the Internet: The Relationship between Internet Communication and Depression, Loneliness, Self-Esteem, and Perceived Social Support," *Cyberpsychology and Behavior* 5, no. 2 (May 2002): 157–71.

8. "Social Media, Social Life: Teens Reveal Their Experiences," Common Sense Media, 2018, https://www.commonsensemedia.org/research/social-media-social-life-2018.

9. Erik Klinenberg, "Is Loneliness a Health Epidemic?" *New York Times*, February 9, 2018, https://www.nytimes.com/2018/02/09/opinion/sunday/loneliness-health.html.

10. Kei Kawashima-Ginsberg and Felicia Sullivan, "Study: 60 Percent of Rural Millennials Lack Access to a Political Life," The Conversation, March 26, 2017, https://theconversation.com/study-60-percent-of-rural-millennials-lack-access-to-a-political-life-74513.

11. Ibid.

12. Matthew N. Atwell, John Bridgeland, and Peter Levine, *Civic Deserts: America's Civic Health Challenge* (Washington, DC: National Conference on Citizenship, 2018), 4, https://www.ncoc.org/wp-content/uploads/2017/10/2017CHIUpdate-FINAL-small.pdf.

13. Kawashima-Ginsberg and Sullivan, "Study: 60 Percent of Rural Millennials."

14. Eric Klinenberg, *Palaces for the People* (New York: Crown, 2018), 37.

15. Quoted in "Lending Library," Benjamin Franklin Historical Society, http://www.benjamin-franklin-history.org/lending-library/.

16. Klinenberg, *Palaces for the People*, 5.

17. Interview with author Andrea Wulf on her book *Founding Gardeners*, by Erin Wayman, "Founding Fathers, Great Gardeners," *Smithsonian Magazine*, August 2011, https://www.smithsonianmag.com/history/founding-fathers-great-gardeners-17209323/.

18. Gregory A. Smith, "Place-Based Education: Learning to be Where We Are," *Phi Delta Kappan* 83, no. 8 (April 2002): 584–94. https://doi.org/10.1177/003172170208300806.

19. Daniel A. Rabuzzi, "Putting the City at the Heart of Place-Based Education," Getting Smart, November 21, 2016, https://www.gettingsmart.com/2016/11/putting-the-city-at-the-heart-of-learning/.

20. Sarah K. Anderson, *Bringing School to Life: Place-Based Education across the Curriculum* (Lanham, MD: Rowman & Littlefield, 2017).

21. Schimmel's quotes from Rebecca Hersher, "All Things Considered: The Conflicting Educations of Sam Schimmel," National Public Radio, May 30, 2018, https://www.npr.org/sections/goatsandsoda/2018/05/30/610384132/the-conflicting-educations-of-sam-schimmel.

10. A VACCINE AGAINST FAKE NEWS

1. "List of Most Popular Websites," *Wikipedia*, last updated April 28, 2019, https://en.wikipedia.org/wiki/List_of_most_popular_websites.

2. Matthew Hindman and Vlad Barash, "Disinformation, 'Fake News' and Influence Campaigns on Twitter," Knight Foundation, October 2018, 3, https://kf-site-production.s3.amazonaws.com/media_elements/files/000/000/238/original/KF-DisinformationReport-final2.pdf.

3. "Fearful of Fake News Blitz, U.S. Census Enlists Help of Tech Giants," NBC News, March 27, 2019, https://www.nbcnews.com/tech/security/fearful-fake-news-blitz-u-s-census-enlists-help-tech-n987821.

4. Nadeem Badshah, "BBC Chief: 'Fake News' Label Erodes Confidence in Journalism," *Guardian*, October 8, 2018, https://www.theguardian.com/media/2018/oct/08/bbc-chief-fake-news-label-erodes-confidence-in-journalism.

5. Michael D. Rich and Jennifer Kavanaugh, *Truth Decay: An Initial Exploration of the Diminishing Role of Facts and Analysis in American Public Life* (Santa Monica, CA: Rand Corporation, 2018), https://www.rand.org/pubs/research_reports/RR2314.html.

6. Ibid., 45–57.

7. "Alternative facts" was a phrase used by White House Counselor to the President Kellyanne Conway in an interview with Chuck Todd on NBC's "Meet the Press," January 22, 2017.

8. Jingjing Jiang, "How Teens and Parents Navigate Screen Time and Device Distractions," Pew Research Center, August 22, 2018, http://www.pewinternet.org/2018/08/22/how-teens-and-parents-navigate-screen-time-and-device-distractions/.

9. Jeffrey Gottfried and Elizabeth Greico, "Younger Americans Are Better than Older Americans at Telling Factual News Statements from Opinions," Pew Research Center, October 23, 2018, http://www.pewresearch.org/fact-tank/2018/10/23/younger-americans-are-better-than-older-americans-at-telling-factual-news-statements-from-opinions/.

10. Stanford History Education Group, Executive Summary of "Evaluating Information: The Cornerstone of Civic Online Reasoning," November 22, 2016, 4, https://stacks.stanford.edu/file/druid:fv751yt5934/SHEG%20Evaluating%20Information%20Online.pdf.

11. Ibid., 10.

12. Ibid., 16.

13. Jackie Zubrzycki, "More States Take on Media Literacy in Schools," *EdWeek*, July 28, 2017, http://blogs.edweek.org/edweek/curriculum/2017/07/media_literacy_laws.html.

14. "Putting Media Literacy on the Public Policy Agenda," Media Literacy Now, February 22, 2019, https://medialiteracynow.org/your-state-legislation/.

15. "What Is Media Literacy?" Media Literacy Now, n.d., https://medialiteracynow.org/what-is-media-literacy/.

16. Ibid.

17. Sam Wineburg and Sarah McGrew, "Lateral Reading and the Nature of Expertise: Reading Less and Learning More When Evaluating Digital Information," *Teachers College Record* 121, no. 11 (2019), https://www.tcrecord.org/Content.asp?ContentId=22806.

18. Ibid., 21.

19. Ibid.

20. Michael A. Caulfield, *Web Literacy for Student Fact-Checkers* (n.p.: Press Books, 2017), can be read for free here: https://webliteracy.pressbooks.com/.

21. Ibid., chapter 2, https://webliteracy.pressbooks.com/chapter/four-strategies/.

22. Ibid, chapter 3, https://webliteracy.pressbooks.com/chapter/building-a-habit-by-checking-your-emotions/.

23. Sarah McGrew, Mark Smith, Joel Breakstone, Teresa Ortega, and Sam Wineburg, "Improving University Students' Web Savvy: An Intervention Study," *British Journal of Educational Psychology*, April 2019, https://doi.org/10.1111/bjep.12279.

24. Michiko Kakutani, *The Death of Truth* (New York: Crown, 2018), 19.

12. LEARNING HOW TO TALK AND LISTEN

1. Jocelyn Kiley, "In Polarized Era, Fewer Americans Hold Mix of Conservative and Liberal Views," Pew Research Center Fact Tank, October 23, 2017, http://www.pewresearch.org/fact-tank/2017/10/23/in-polarized-era-fewer-americans-hold-a-mix-of-conservative-and-liberal-views/.

2. Carroll Doherty and Jocelyn Kiley, "Key Facts about Partisanship and Animosity in America," Pew Research Center Fact Tank, June 22, 2016, http://www.pewresearch.org/fact-tank/2016/06/22/key-facts-partisanship/.

3. Eric Liu, "Americans Don't Need Reconciliation—They Need to Get Better at Arguing," *Atlantic Monthly*, November 1, 2016, https://www.theatlantic.com/politics/archive/2016/11/post-election-reconciliation/506027/. "Truth and reconciliation" is a phrase taken from South Africa's dismantling of apartheid.

4. Aspen Institute of Citizenship and American Identity and Facing History and Ourselves, *What Is a Better Argument?: The Better Arguments Project Report on Key Operating Principles*, March 2018, 7–9, https://assets.aspeninstitute.org/content/uploads/2018/03/Better-Arguments-Report-Cover_FINAL.pdf.

5. Quoted in Kelly Swanson, "Experts Agree: Don't Avoid Political Conversations with Family Members," Vox, August 22, 2017, https://www.vox.com/first-person/2017/8/22/16171270/partisanship-politics-discussion-family.

6. Diana Hess, *Controversy in the Classroom: The Democratic Power of Discussion* (New York: Routledge, 2009).

7. Diana E. Hess and Paula McAvoy, *The Political Classroom: Evidence and Ethics in Democratic Education* (New York: Routledge, 2015), 5.

8. Excerpt of Professor Joshua Dunn's essay in *Talking Out of Turn: Teacher Speech for Hire* (edited by Meira Levinson, to be published in 2019) is taken from a blog post by Robert Pondiscio, "Teachers, Curb Your Activism," Thomas H. Fordham Institute, October 24, 2018, https://fordhaminstitute.org/national/commentary/teachers-curb-your-activism.

9. Kushner quoted in Hess and McAvoy, *The Political Classroom*, 115–16.

10. Ibid., 58.

11. Kyra Gurney, "Last Fall, They Debated Gun Control in Class. Now, They Debate Lawmakers on TV," *Miami Herald*, February 23, 2018, https://www.miamiherald.com/news/local/education/article201678544.html.

12. Robert E. Litan, "A Counterintuitive Proposal for Improving Education and Healing America: Debate-Centered Instruction," Brown Center Chalkboard at the Brookings Institute, September 27, 2018, https://www.brookings.edu/blog/brown-center-chalkboard/2018/09/27/a-counterintuitive-proposal-for-improving-education-and-healing-america-debate-centered-instruction/.

13. Briana Mezuk, Irina Bondarenko, Suzanne Smith, and Eric Tucker, "Impact of Participating in Policy Debate Program on Academic Achievement: Evidence from the Chicago Urban Debate League," *Educational Research and Reviews* 6, no. 9 (September 2011): 622–35, http://www.socialimpactexchange.org/sites/www.socialimpactexchange.org/files/Third%20Party%20Evaluation,%20Education%20Research%20and%20Reviews.pdf.

13. THE FUTURE'S CITIZEN

1. Edwin's last name has been omitted at the request of his family.

2. Mikva Challenge is another action civics nonprofit out of Chicago. See https://www.mikvachallenge.org/.

3. Matthew N. Atwell, John Bridgeland, and Peter Levine, *Civic Deserts: America's Civic Health Challenge* (Washington, DC: National Conference on Citizenship, 2018), https://www.ncoc.org/wp-content/uploads/2017/10/2017CHIUpdate-FINAL-small.pdf. See also the discussion in chapter 8.

4. Atwell, Bridgeland, and Levine, *Civic Deserts*, 27.

5. Kei Kawashima-Ginsberg and Felicia Sullivan, "Study: 60 Percent of Rural Millennials Lack Access to a Political Life," The Conversation, March 26, 2017, https://theconversation.com/study-60-percent-of-rural-millennials-lack-access-to-a-political-life-74513.

6. Shira Shoenberg, "Governor Charlie Baker Amends Massachusetts Civics Bill to Keep It Non-Partisan," MassLive, August 3, 2018, https://www.masslive.com/politics/index.ssf/2018/08/gov_charlie_baker_amends_civic.html.

7. John Muresianu, "Civics Education Should Focus on Critical Thinking, Not Activism," Real Clear Education, September 11, 2018, https://www.realcleareducation.com/articles/2018/09/11/civics_education_should_focus_on_critical_thinkingnot_activism.html.

8. Ibid.

9. Ibid.

10. Statistics from the Mikva Challenge website homepage, 2018, https://www.mikvachallenge.org/.

11. Generation Citizen, *2017–2018 Impact Progress Report*, 3, https://generationcitizen.org/wp-content/uploads/2018/11/FY18-Impact-Progress-Report-28129.pdf.

12. Question taken from Diana E. Hess and Paula McAvoy, *The Political Classroom: Evidence and Ethics in Democratic Education* (New York: Routledge, 2015), 5.

Index

ACEs. *See* adverse childhood experiences
action civics, xvii, 38, 119, 130–131;
 Baker push back and amendment on,
 128; civic knowledge and skills and
 dispositions building in, 127; in civics,
 new, 13, 15, 17, 27, 33; Curran "a-ha"
 moment in, 123; democracy's essential
 question in, 130; democratic values
 defending in, 127; education movement
 in, 127–128; Generation Citizen
 curriculum implementation of, 121;
 "informed action" projects in, 128;
 Muresianu on critical thinking and
 student example in, 128–129; Rhodes
 on, 126–127; rural districts practical
 concerns in, 124; short-term surveys on,
 129; students as change agents in, 127;
 top down and bottom up working of,
 130; Warren on, 130
action civics class: class time loss in, 126;
 identification forms and license fees
 changing of, 126; immigration issues
 work in, 125; Oklahoma driver's
 licenses bill and public reaction in, 125;
 Oklahoma State Capitol building Civics
 Day for, 126; Rhodes concerns about,
 126
adverse childhood experiences (ACEs), 62
Alaska, 103, 104
American Historical Association, 51

Andrew, Seth, 15, 36, 38, 130; action
 civics worry of, 38; civics innovation
 and, 37; "civic success sequence" of,
 38, 40; democracy exposure and, 38;
 Democracy Prep charter school of, 36,
 40; on history and government
 understanding, 37; politics and
 government revelations of, 35–36; as
 politics kid, 35; Rhode Island state
 representative campaign of, 35; on
 skills and dispositions, 37; U.S.
 citizenship test and, 37
Annenberg Public Policy Center, xiii
Antey, Amanda: on Evansville
 disengagement, 87; political "powder
 keg" concern of, 87; on political
 silence, 87; on Young Voices as civic
 engagement, 88; Young Voices
 sponsoring of, 87
Arendt, Hannah, 91
arguments, 107, 109; collaborative
 relationships in, 112; context matters in,
 112; engagement and transformation in,
 112; five principles of better, 111–112;
 listening in, 111; Pew Research study
 on, 111; push and pull of, 111;
 reckoning before reconciliation in, 111;
 trust and vulnerability in, 112; young
 people political discussions
 discouragement and, 112

globalization and, xvi; Jefferson on knowledgeable citizens, xii; Jennings on, 32; Lincoln on, 20; Mann on, 20; Massachusetts bill on, 32, 33; media literacy and character education in, xvii; NAEP report on gaps in, xiii, 25; parents as teachers of, 33; racial and economic learning gaps in, 25; revival in, xvii; schools stop teaching of, xii; semester's worth of, 23; "space race" and protest movements impacting, 22; standards-based education reform movement altering, 22–23; state bills expanding, 27–28; state-by-state requirements for, 28, 31, 33; teacher concerns about, xvi; teachers new projects for, xviii; Thomas B. Fordham Institute review of, xii–xiii, 23; three branches of government study in, xii; twenty-first century change in, xvii; unequal distribution of, 23, 33; U.S. citizenship test use in, 28; year of research in, xv; young people preparation in, xii

civics education, six proven practices of, 12, 28, 118, 130; current events and controversial issues discussion as, 12–13; democratic process and adult civic roles simulations as, 13, 25; extracurricular activities in, 13; school governance student participation as, 13; service learning in, 13; social studies classroom instruction as, 12

climate change: in Alaska, 103; Alaska Youth for Environmental Action lawsuit and, 104; Baring civic discourse avenues pursuit of, 104; Baring constant learning about, 103–104; Baring declaration and, 104; Baring on activism in, 105; Baring on reality of, 103; fossil fuel industry dismissal attempt in, 104; Ninth Circuit Court of Appeals decision on, 104–105; oil revenues competing with, 104; public support in, 105; Supreme Court ruling in, 105

Climate Change Research Group, International Arctic Research Center, 103

The Coddling of the American Mind (Haidt and Lukianoff), 6

"common schools" movement, 20, 21

Common Sense Media, 57, 76

Community High School, West Chicago, Illinois: civic knowledge gap narrowing at, 25; history requirements at, 24; racially and economically diverse population of, 24; senior government class first day at, 24; state legislative session simulation of, 24; student representatives and bill passing in, 24; tracking resistance at, 24

Core Virtues curriculum: American courage stories as basis for, 63–64; Klee creation of, 64; rich language use in, 64; self focus absence in, 65; shared humanity and, 65; specific vocabulary use in, 64–65; virtues rotating list use in, 64; Washington courage story in, 63; young people inspiring in, 64

Corin, Jaclyn, xi

Costello, Maureen, 58

CRAAP. *See* Currency, Relevance, Authority, Accuracy, and Purpose

critical thinking, 9, 11, 47, 51, 97, 101, 128–129

Cruz, Alan, 3

Curran, Amy, 121; action civics "a-ha" moment of, 123; Generation Citizen meeting attending of, 122; Generation Citizen school curriculum recruitment of, 123; on geographic civic engagement gap, 124; kids' elementary school saving of, 122; multiple roadblocks of, 123; school funding research of, 122

Currency, Relevance, Authority, Accuracy, and Purpose (CRAAP), 97

DACA. *See* Deferred Action for Childhood Arrivals

Dalai Lama, 65

DBQ. *See* Document-Based Questions Project

The Death of Truth (Kakutani), 100, 101

debate, 118; argue both sides preparation in, 117; crucial skills knowledge in, 116, 118; digital technology enhancing,

91–92; "talk" tab and links in, 92
Wineburg, Sam, 91–92, 94, 95–96, 97–98, 99–100
Wu, Olivia, 2
Wunn, Scott, 116–117, 118

Young Voices, 88, 89; all political persuasions in, 89; at Castle High School, 87, 88; as civic engagement, 88
You're More Powerful Than You Think (Liu), 2
YouTube, 4, 58

Zeiger, Hans, 27

About the Author

Holly Korbey writes about education and parenting, often exploring the intersection of teachers, parents, and schools, and how students learn. In addition to the new civics education, she has written about how the arts influence learning, how social-emotional learning plays out in classrooms, and what happened when she decided not to "redshirt" her kindergarten-aged son. Korbey's work on how dyslexia is handled (and often mishandled) in schools was nominated for an Education Writers Association award. The *New York Times*, *Atlantic Monthly*, *KQED MindShift*, Edutopia, *Bright* magazine, *Brain*, *Child* magazine, and other outlets have published her stories, and she regularly speaks to groups of parents and educators on topics of teaching and learning. She lives in Nashville, Tennessee, with her husband and three sons, and can usually be found reading a book at Little League practice. Visit her online at hollykorbey.com. This is her first book.